Insider Guide

Ace Your Case® IV: The Latest and Greatest

2004 Edition

D1608324

Helping you make smarter career decisions.

WetFeet Inc.

609 Mission Street
Suite 400
San Francisco, CA 94105

Phone: (415) 284-7900 or 1-800-926-4JOB
Fax: (415) 284-7910
E-mail: info@wetfeet.com
Website: www.wetfeet.com

Ace Your Case® IV: The Latest and Greatest

ISBN: 1-58207-367-8

Table of Contents

Nailing the Case 51

Ace Your Case IV at a Glance

Case-by-Case Rules

Here's a summary of the different types of cases you'll find in this report, along with some rules that should help you ace your answer.

Market-Sizing Questions

- *Use round numbers.*
- *Show your work.*
- *Use paper and calculator.*

Business Operations Questions

- *Isolate the main issue.*
- *Apply a framework.*
- *Think "action."*

Business Strategy Questions

- *Think frameworks.*
- *Ask questions.*
- *Work from big to small.*

Resume Cases

- *Know your story*
- *Keep the Parent Test in mind.*
- *Let your excitement shine!*

The Interview Unplugged

- Overview

- The Case Interview

Overview

When it comes to preparing for your case interviews, there's one word and one word only: practice. By now, you're spending all of your spare time thinking about why Dell is getting into printers, why the utility industry is consolidating, and how much mustard is consumed in Idaho. Your family thinks you're an oddball, but you're on the right track. You're probably even starting to enjoy thinking about these issues. Watch out: You might be turning into a consultant.

This guide is designed to be a companion volume to *Ace Your Case!*, *Ace Your Case II,* and *Ace Your Case III.* It offers new detailed explanations about different case types and more sample questions. Many of our sample case questions here are based on real, live case questions that people received in their interviews last year.

For those who haven't seen our other case-interviewing guides, *Ace Your Case!* discusses the consulting interview in general and offers a primer containing a number of common frameworks and B-school-type tools (watch out for the 3Cs and the 4Ps, not to mention the infamous Five Forces) that should help you attack your case questions. *Ace Your Case II* and *Ace Your Case III* each contain 15 specific case questions and detailed recommended answers, as does this edition.

A word about how to use this guide: We strongly recommend that you try to solve the questions first, without looking at the answers. After you've given them your best shot, go ahead and check out our recommended answers. If you find that our "good answer" differs from yours, see if there's something you can learn from our suggestions. But don't panic—there are usually

numerous ways to answer any case question. It's far more important to note the approach, as well as the interviewer's likely responses, which obviously won't be included in your own answers. As you sharpen those skills, keep thinking to yourself, "I love these case questions!" Pretty soon you'll find yourself talking like a consultant!

The Case Interview

Background

Many management consulting firms, especially the strategy firms (McKinsey, The Boston Consulting Group, Bain, Mercer, and others) love to give prospective employees a problem to solve during the course of the interview. These problem-solving exercises, known generally as "case questions," are designed to help the interviewer screen candidates and determine which people really have what it takes to be a real, live, card-carrying management consultant.

Case questions come in many forms and levels of complexity. To help you get a handle on them, we have identified four different categories of questions:

- *Market-sizing questions*
- *Business operations questions*
- *Business strategy questions*
- *Resume questions*

(Note that we are not covering the brainteaser category in this Insider Guide. Consulting firms rarely ask brainteaser questions; other types of cases give much more insight into the type of thinking that makes a good consultant.)

Each of these prototypes has certain distinguishing features, which we discuss below. In addition, our insiders recommend certain "rules of the road" that should help you successfully navigate the different types of questions. Don't worry-you'll never be asked to spit out a category name and serial number for the questions you receive in the interview. Nevertheless, if you can identify the type of question, you will have a better idea about how to effectively attack the problem.

What Your Interviewer Is Seeking

It may seem as if your interviewer is using the case technique for one purpose alone: to humiliate prospective consultants. Although a few interviewers do seem to take a perverse pleasure in watching candidates writhe, this isn't the true goal of the technique. According to insiders, case questions really do help interviewers evaluate a candidate's aptitude for consulting. What does that mean exactly? Whether you're an undergrad, an MBA, or a PhD, consulting interviewers will likely depend on the case questions to check you out on the following dimensions:

- Analytical ability
- Intelligence
- Ability to not break into hives under pressure
- Common sense
- Ability to think on your feet
- Interest in problem solving
- Business intuition

- Facility with numbers
- Presentation skills
- Communication skills
- Ability to sort through information and focus on the key points
- Ability to analyze and then make recommendations based on the analysis
- Creativity
- Enthusiasm

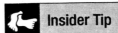

Insider Tip

Try to make the interview more of a dialogue between equals. Try to have fun.

Before you bid all your points to get an interview with name-your-consulting-firm, we recommend that you spend some time thinking about how consulting fits you. In particular, you must have good answers to two questions: Why do you want to be a consultant? And why do you want to work for this firm?

If you have good answers to these two questions, then you're ready to start thinking about cases. We start by discussing the case interview as it relates to several categories of candidates: undergraduates, MBAs, advanced-degree candidates, and experienced hires.

Undergraduates

Consulting interviewers tell us that the case questions and the expected answers for undergraduates tend to be simpler and more understandable than those for MBA students. Market-sizing questions are very popular (you will almost certainly get at least one of these), as are general business strategy problems. In the business strategy area, the companies and the topics may also seem a little more friendly; you're more likely to get a case about a beer company than about a company trying to license the latest packet-filtering technology for data encryption. Operations questions (with the exception of the ever-popular

declining-profits question) are less common for undergraduates, and resume questions will more likely focus on academic or extracurricular activities than on work experiences.

Interviewers tell us that they often provide more prompting to undergraduate candidates during the interview. In evaluating your answer to a question, only the most sadistic interviewer would expect you to regurgitate all of the standard business-school terminology and techniques (after all, how else could the company justify paying MBAs the big bucks?). But beware: Rank amateurs are definitely not welcome. Thus, you must have a general understanding of basic business relationships (e.g. revenues - costs = profits), but don't get your knickers in a knot if you can't name even one of the Five Forces.

Here are a few real, live case questions fielded by our undergraduate customers:

- How many jelly beans would it take to fill a 747?
- Your client is the owner of a hip sushi restaurant and bar in New York. The place is always packed, but it isn't profitable. What's going on?
- Two prominent hospitals are planning a merger. What are some of the issues they should think about?

MBAs

MBAs have long been the heavy hitters of the consulting workforce. As a result, the case interview reaches its most sophisticated and demanding form in the MBA interview. All types of questions—from the simple market-sizer to the gnarliest of business strategy problems—are fair game. Practically any industry or functional issue area is possible material for the case question. An MBA candidate will be expected to be familiar with a number of the standard MBA frameworks and concepts. Also, the case will possibly have a few tricky twists or turns. For example, what might seem like a pure and simple international strategy question might be complicated by an unexpected restriction related to the European regulatory environment.

Interviewers tell us that most MBAs have a polished interview technique and understand the basics of many case problems. Therefore, they look for depth in the answer (what they describe as an ability to peel the onion and a real familiarity with business concepts. We understand that at least some recruiters like to ask resume case questions because they provide an opportunity to get more detail about the candidate's background and problem-solving experiences.

Here are a few real, live case questions fielded by our MBA customers:

- How many diapers are sold in the United States in a year?
- An online brokerage is contemplating expansion into additional financial services categories. Should it go ahead with the expansion?
- A sunglasses manufacturer discovers that its costs are far above industry average. What should it do?

Advanced-Degree Candidates (Non-MBAs)

Although consulting firms are attracting record numbers of MBA applicants, several of the top firms have started to look beyond traditional feeder programs to identify top talent. According to WetFeet customers and recruiters, the different firms have very different approaches to advanced-degree candidates. McKinsey and BCG, among others, have launched aggressive recruiting programs aimed at PhDs, MDs, JDs, and others at the top schools. In the process, some of these firms have created customized recruiting and training programs for advanced-degree candidates. Other firms continue to consider advanced-degree candidates on a case-by-case basis, often pitting them against undergraduate or MBA candidates, depending on their background.

If you enter a separate recruiting track, you will, according to our customers, still have to contend with interviews that are similar in format to that of undergraduate and MBA recruiting programs. In other words, expect a heavy dose of case interview questions along with the general get-to-know-you

queries. One slight difference is that, in addition to seeing whether you can handle the substance of the case question, the recruiter will also be looking to see "if [you] can break out of the PhD box." In other words, can you adapt to the real world and answer questions without giving too much detail?

According to WetFeet customers, case questions for advanced-degree candidates usually don't require you to carry your own MBA toolbox. Instead, the questions may relate to previous research (your resume is usually a font of material), or they may resemble undergraduate case studies that check a person's intuition, common sense, analytical skills, and problem-solving abilities. Interviewers at various top firms say they may be more inclined to prompt candidates with questions, and they may be satisfied with a good, solid analytical answer that doesn't necessarily incorporate all of the latest business buzzwords.

Check out these case questions fielded by our advanced-degree customers:

- How many taxicabs are there in New York City?
- A winery has hired you to tell it why it has been experiencing declining profits.
- Question for someone who studied physics: What has been the most important development in the field of physics in the last five years?

Experienced Hires

If you are seeking to join a consulting firm from industry, or from another consulting firm, your interviewing experience may differ from that described in this report. According to WetFeet customers, experienced-hire candidates may or may not face a battery of case questions. There is no hard-and-fast rule, but it seems as though people with more experience (ten-plus years), and people who have already worked for a name-brand consulting firm, are relatively unlikely to face a case as part of their review process. In contrast, people who

have worked in industry for a few years and who are seeking to enter at a middle level are likely to go through a process similar to that used for MBAs (i.e. expect lots of cases). In particular, if you are changing careers (e.g. moving from non-profit work to consulting) and not signing on as an industry authority, you'll probably be scrutinized for your consulting aptitude—as demonstrated by your ability to field case questions.

Typical case questions faced by our experienced-hire customers include:

- Your client is a struggling telecom firm. How would you turn it around?
- Your client is a U.S.-based company that sells telephones by mail. Mail sales of telephones are a small portion of the company's overall business, and sales are below average for mail-order sales of appliances. Should the client continue to sell phones in this way? If so, how should it make the operation more profitable?
- Specific questions related to their area of expertise.

Company-Specific Variations

As you enter the ring with consultants from a variety of firms, you'll probably notice differences in the questions you receive, as well as the style and approach of the case interview. More often than not, these differences derive from the differences in the personalities and experiences of your interviewers. However, several firms have developed their own approach to the case interview. One variation involves giving a candidate a written case prior to the interview and asking him or her to prepare to discuss the case in detail during the interview. We understand that PricewaterhouseCoopers (now IBM Business Consulting Services) and Monitor Group have given preprinted cases to candidates before an interview. Monitor has also used a group interview technique that requires competing candidates to work with each other to solve a problem, while McKinsey has been experimenting with a process for undergraduates that includes both a written case test and a group interview.

One other thing to keep in mind: Recruiters suggest that you would be wise to keep the firm's reputation and areas of strength in mind as you launch into your case answer. Firms that are known for a particular type of work are likely to be more sensitive to those issues in the case questions they give. For example, if you're interviewing with Towers Perrin, you shouldn't be surprised to find a "people issue" somewhere in the case. If you're talking with Deloitte Consulting, keep "operations" in mind as you craft an answer—and don't talk about how it's important to work only with the company's top management. And, if you're interviewing with Bain, remember how much importance the company attaches to "measurable results" and "data-driven" analysis.

Case-by-Case Rules

- Market-Sizing Case

- Business Operations Cases

- Business Strategy Cases

- Resume Cases

Market-Sizing Cases

Overview

Consultants love to ask market-sizing questions. Not only are they easy to create, discuss, and evaluate, they are also highly representative of an important type of work done by consultants. In their simplest form, market-sizing cases require the candidate to determine the size of a particular market (hence the name). In the real world, this information can be especially helpful when gauging the attractiveness of a new market. In the interview context, a market-sizing question might be pitched in an extremely straightforward manner (e.g. "What is the market for surfboards in the United States?"). Or it may be disguised as a more complex question (e.g. "Do you think Fidelity should come out with a mutual fund targeted at high-net worth individuals?") that requires the respondent to peel away the extraneous detail in order to identify the market-sizing issue at the core. In a more highly developed variation, the interviewer might ask a strategy or operations case question that requires the respondent to do some market-sizing in order to come up with an appropriate recommendation.

The Scorecard

Market-sizing questions allow the interviewer to test the candidate's facility with numbers, powers of analysis, and common sense. For example, if you were asked to size the surfboard market, you would need to make basic assumptions about the market. (How many people surf? How many boards does a typical surfer dude or gal own? How often will he or she get a new one? Are there

other big purchasers besides individual surfers? Is there a market for used boards?) You would also need to make a few basic calculations (number of surfers $\times$ number of new boards per year + total quantity purchased by other types of customers, etc.). As you work through these issues, the interviewer would also get a glimpse of your common sense. (Did you assume that everybody in the U.S. population would be a potential surfer, or did you try to estimate the population in prime surfing areas like California and Hawaii?)

We get the 'deer in the headlights' look from time to time. That's an automatic ding.

Location

Market-sizing questions can pop up in all interviews. They are almost certain to make an appearance in undergraduate and advanced-degree interviews. Indeed, both undergraduates and PhDs report receiving exactly the same market-sizing questions in their respective interviews. MBAs are also likely to receive market-sizing questions; however, a common and more complex variation typical of an MBA interview involves assessing the opportunity for a new product. For example, you might be asked whether your pharmaceutical company client should develop and market a drug for male pattern baldness. Part of the analysis would require you to estimate the market potential (i.e. market size) for the drug.

Manhandling Your Market-Sizing Questions

Market-sizing questions can intimidate. But once you understand the rules (and practice your technique), you can come to view these cases as slow pitches right over the center of the plate. So, just how many golf balls are used in the United States in a year? You don't know, and the truth is, neither does your interviewer.

In fact, your interviewer doesn't even care what the real number is. But remember, she does care about your ability to use logic, common sense, and creativity to get to a plausible answer. And she wants to make sure you don't turn tail when you've got a few numbers to run. Which brings us to the three rules for market-sizing questions.

Rule 1: Use round numbers. Even if you weren't a multivariate calculus stud, you can impress your interviewer with your number-crunching abilities if you stick to round numbers. They're much easier to add, subtract, multiply, and divide, and since we've already decided that the exact answer doesn't matter anyway, go ahead and pick something that you can toss around with ease. Good examples? One hundred, one million, ten dollars, two, one-half. The population of New York City? Ten million, give or take.

Rule 2: Show your work. Case questions are the ultimate "show your work" questions. In fact, your exact answer matters less than the path you took to get there. Remember, the market-sizing question is merely a platform through which your interviewer can test your analysis, creativity, and comfort with numbers.

Rule 3: Use paper and calculator. If you feel more comfortable writing everything down and using a calculator, do! Most interviewers will not care if you use a pencil and paper to keep your thoughts organized and logical. And if pulling out the HP to multiply a few numbers keeps you from freaking out, then by all means do it. Your interviewer will be more impressed if you are calm, cool, and collected, and if using props helps you, then go for it.

Business Operations Cases

Overview

A fair number of case questions cover operations issues. Given the existing economic environment, the mix of consulting business has shifted more towards operations and process-focused cases, so be prepared for at least one of these types of questions. Broadly speaking, "operations" refers to everything that's involved in running a business and getting product out the door. In a manufacturing plant, this would include the purchasing and transporting of raw materials, the manufacturing processes, the scheduling of staff and facilities, the distribution of the product, the servicing of equipment in the field, and so on. In its broadest sense, operations would even include the sales and marketing of the company's products and the systems used to track sales. Whereas strategy questions deal with the future direction of the firm (e.g. whether to enter a new line of business), operations deals with the day-to-day running of the business. It is a particularly fertile ground for consulting work, and for case questions. Some of the most typical case questions of this type are those that require the candidate to explain why a company's sales or profits have declined.

The Scorecard

Consultants like to ask operations questions because they allow the interviewer to see whether the candidate understands fundamental issues related to running a business (e.g. the relationship between revenues and costs, and the relationship and impact of fixed costs and variable costs on a company's profitability). In addition, operations questions require the candidate to

demonstrate a good grasp of process and an ability to sort through a pile of information and identify the most important factors.

Location

Operations questions are fair game for all candidates, including undergraduates and advanced-degree candidates. According to our customers, the "declining profits" questions are some of the most popular types of cases around, and almost all candidates can expect to get at least one of these. That said, MBAs are typically expected to explore these questions in greater detail and have a better grasp of key business issues and terminology. MBAs could also get tossed more complicated operations questions. For example, an MBA case might involve understanding the implications of allocating fixed costs in a certain way, or, perhaps, the impact on the balance sheet of a certain type of financing. Undergraduates and non-MBA candidates still need to be familiar with a few basic operational concepts, such as the relationship between costs and revenues, and the various things that might have an impact on them. In addition, undergraduates might expect that the topic of the question be more familiar. For example, an undergraduate might get lobbed a question about the implications of launching a new national chain of restaurants. An MBA might get a question about factors that would allow a manufacturing operation to increase throughput.

Optimizing Your Business Operations Answers

Operations case questions are more complex than market-sizing questions. Not only do they typically require basic business knowledge (or, at the very least, a good deal of common sense), but they also frequently require the candidate to think like a detective. For example, the interviewer might ask why an airline has been losing money while its market share has increased. There could be many

reasons for this: Revenues might be down (and that, in turn, might be caused by any number of things, including ticket price wars, lower ridership, growing accounts payable, and so on); costs might be higher (due to higher fuel costs, greater landing fees, higher plane maintenance costs, and other factors); or the airline could be operating more inefficiently (e.g. higher passenger loads might require it to lease additional aircraft or pay staff overtime). In any case, a successful analysis of the question requires the candidate to think clearly and efficiently about the question. To help with these types of questions, here are some rules you'll want to keep in mind:

Rule 1: Isolate the main issue. Operations questions usually have lots of potential answers. The first step in identifying a good answer (and demonstrating your analytical firepower) is to separate the wheat from the chaff. Once you've zeroed in on the main issue, you'll be able to apply your energy to working out a good conclusion to the problem.

Rule 2: Apply a framework. Frameworks were made for cracking operations questions. They will help you sift through lots of data and organize your answer. A useful framework can be something as simple as saying, "If the airline is losing money, it has something to do with either costs or revenues," and moving on to talk about each of these areas in turn.

Rule 3: Think action! Unlike your market-sizing question, operations questions never end with a nice, neat analysis. Rather, the goal here is action. The hypothetical client is usually facing a critical issue: Revenues are falling, costs are rising, production is crashing. Something needs to be done. As a consultant, you will be hired to give advice. As a candidate, you should be sensitive to the fact that your analysis must drive toward a solution. Even if you need more data before you're able to make a final recommendation, you should acknowledge that you are evaluating various courses of action. Better yet, you should lay out a plan for next steps.

Business Strategy Cases

Case-by-Case Rules

Overview

Business strategy cases are the granddaddies (and demons) of the case question world. Consultants love to use these questions because they touch on so many different issues. A good strategy question can have a market-sizing piece, a logic puzzle, multiple operations issues, and a major dose of creativity and action thrown in for good measure. Moreover, a complex strategy question can go in many different directions, thereby allowing the interviewer to probe the candidate's abilities in a variety of areas. Again, strategy case questions can run the gamut from a complex, multi-industry, multinational, multi-issue behemoth to a localized question with a pinpoint focus.

The Scorecard

Depending on the nature of the question, the interviewer can use it to assess anything and everything from your ability to handle numbers to your ability to wade through a mass of detailed information and synthesize it into a compelling business strategy. Of all the different types of case questions, these are also the most similar to the actual work you'll do on the job (at least at the strategy firms). One other thing the interviewer will be checking carefully: your presentation skills.

Location

Strategy case questions are fair game for any type of candidate. For undergraduates, they will often be more two-dimensional and straightforward.

For MBA candidates, they frequently have several layers of issues, and perhaps an international or other twist to boot. Although most strategy boutiques will use this kind of case as a mainstay in their recruiting efforts, firms with more of an operations focus may rely more heavily on operations questions.

Succeeding at the Strategy Stumpers

Because business strategy questions can involve many different elements, they may inspire fear in the weak of heart. Although it's true that strategy questions can be the most difficult, they can also be the most fun. This is your opportunity to play CEO, or at least advisor to the CEO. You can put all of your business intuition and your hard-nosed, data-driven research to work and come up with a plan that will bring a huge multinational corporation into the limelight—or not. Does it matter that you just crafted a story about why a credit-card company should go into the Italian market when your best friend who interviewed immediately prior to you recommended against going Italian? No, not really. Unless, of course, your friend did a better job of exploring the case question. What does that mean? By going through this book (and the other WetFeet *Ace Your Case* guides), you're already a step ahead of the game. However, here are the rules you'll want to keep in mind as you tackle your strategy case questions.

Rule 1: Think frameworks. While analyzing a really juicy strategy question you might be able to draw information and jargon out of almost every course in your school's core business curriculum. Don't succumb to temptation! Your interviewer will be much more impressed by a clear and simple story about how you are attacking the question and where you are going with your analysis. The best way to do this is to apply a framework to the problem. As with operations questions, this means setting out a plan of attack up front and following it through to conclusion. One other big benefit: Having a clear framework will help you organize your analysis.

Rule 2: Ask questions. Successful consulting is as much about asking the right questions as it is about providing a good answer. Likewise, your solution to a strategy case will be much better if you've focused your energy on the right issue. To help you get there, don't hesitate to ask your interviewer questions. In the best case, he may help you avoid a derailment; in the worst case, he'll understand your thought process as you plow through the analysis.

Rule 3: Work from big to small. Even though the strategy case you are examining was the subject of a study that lasted several months, you probably have about 15 minutes to provide your answer. Therefore it's essential that you start by looking at the most significant issues first. Besides, this is a great discipline for future consultants; the client may be paying for your time by the hour, so you'll want to make sure that you really are adding value.

Resume Cases

Overview

One favorite type of alternative case question is the resume case. Instead of cooking up a case question based on a carefully disguised project from his files, the interviewer will pull something straight from the candidate's resume. Usually, these cases stem from a previous professional experience, but occasionally you'll get something like: "I see you play rugby. Describe for me all of the different positions on a rugby team, and the play strategy for each." Frequently, the interviewer will ask the candidate to walk through a previous

work project or experience and explain how he or she decided on a particular course of action. As the candidate goes through the discussion, the interviewer may then change a few critical assumptions and ask the candidate to explain how he or she would have responded. For example, if you had started and run a successful computer repair service, the interviewer might ask how you would have responded if a local computer store had created a knock-off service and offered it at a lower price.

The Scorecard

The resume case is a way for the interviewer to dig a little deeper into your resume and at the same time test your case-cracking capabilities. (It also adds a little variety to a grueling day of interviews.) Here, the interviewer is testing for your ability to communicate—in layman's terms—a topic that is very familiar to you. Resume cases are generally a good opportunity for you to toot your own horn a bit about your past experience and exude confidence, competence, and enthusiasm about things you really understand.

Location

The resume question is fair game for undergrads, MBAs, and advanced-degree candidates. Naturally, because the resumes for each type of candidate differ significantly, the types of questions also differ. MBAs can expect business-oriented questions; advanced-degree candidates can expect questions related to their previous research. PhD students tell us that they commonly receive resume cases. Not only do resume cases allow the candidate to avoid feeling like he or she has to master a whole new lexicon and body of frameworks, they test his or her communications skills.

Rocking Your Resume Case

Because the resume case question takes the discussion to your home turf, there isn't really a secret recipe for pulling apart the question. Rather, the way to be successful here is to follow a few basic interview rules.

Rule 1: Know your story. Nothing will make you look worse—and help you find the door more quickly—than not knowing what you put on your own resume. Make sure you've reviewed all of the items on your resume before the interview. Write down a few notes about what you did at each job, and the main message you want to convey through each bullet point on your resume. Think up a short story for each bullet point that will provide compelling evidence to support those messages.

Rule 2: Keep the Parent Test in mind. This is not the place to play the polyglot; nobody will be impressed with your ability to speak techno-babble. The interviewer will assume that you know everything there is to know about your area of expertise, whether that's molecular biology or your computer-repair service. The real question is can you tell others about what you did without sending them into a coma? It may sound easy, but many people seem incapable of communicating what they know. Our suggestion? Practice talking about your work as if you were telling your parents all about it.

Rule 3: Let your excitement shine. This is your home field, so use it to your advantage. Talk about your past work with energy and enthusiasm. Believe it or not, even consultants like a little passion. Besides, if you're sitting there griping about a previous work experience, guess what's running through your interviewer's mind: "Whoa, Nelly. This cat could be trouble!"

The Practice Range

- Market-Sizing Case Questions

- Business Operations Case Questions

- Business Strategy Case Questions

- Resume Case Questions

Market-Sizing Questions

Remember the rules for market-sizing questions:

1. Use round numbers.

2. Show your work.

3. Use paper and calculator.

How many golf carts are there in the United States?

Key questions to ask:

_____

_____

_____

_____

Basic equations/numbers:

_____

_____

_____

How you'd track the numbers down:

_____

_____

_____

How long does it take a Starbucks to serve enough coffee to completely fill the gas tank of a Hummer?

Key questions to ask:

_____

_____

_____

Basic equations/numbers:

_____

_____

_____

How you'd track the numbers down:

_____

_____

_____

The Practice Range

Having fallen on hard times, your consulting firm has decided to serve a notorious bank robber. He has asked you to determine how many briefcases he must bring with him in order to steal $10 million in cash, all $100 bills, in bundles of 1,000 bills each.

Key questions to ask:

_____

_____

_____

Basic equations/numbers:

_____

_____

_____

How you'd track the numbers down:

_____

_____

_____

CASE 4

How many unique horse jockeys ride in races in the United States on an average Saturday?

Key questions to ask:

_____

_____

_____

_____

Basic equations/numbers:

_____

_____

_____

How you'd track the numbers down:

_____

_____

_____

Business Operations Questions

Remember the rules for business operations questions:

1. Isolate the main issue.

2. Apply a framework.

3. Think action!

CASE 5

The general manager of a popular ski resort has called on you to help her figure out why her resort has been experiencing declining profits over the past three years. How would you help her?

Key questions to ask:

_____

_____

_____

Basic equations/numbers:

_____

_____

_____

How you'd track the numbers down:

_____

_____

_____

CASE 6

Your client is a publisher of romance novels that sells to retail bookstores. The standard arrangement in the industry is that publishers must reimburse their customers at the end of the year for any unsold inventory. In this case, you are to assume that any inventory that is sent back to the publisher must be destroyed and has no resale value. One of your client's customers has made a proposal: for a 10 percent discount on wholesale prices, they will no longer send back any books at the end of the year. Should the publisher do the deal? The following data exists:

- In 2002, the client sold 10,000 books to the bookstore.
- Client's production facilities are partially self-owned domestic, and partially contracted to overseas vendors, primarily in Asia.
- The average wholesale price of a book in 2002 was $10.
- It costs the client $5 on average to make a single book.
- The romance novel segment of the publishing industry has been flat for almost a decade, and is expected to remain so in coming years.
- In 2002, the bookstore sent back 20 percent of its order to the client at the end of the year.

Key questions to ask:

_____

_____

_____

_____

The Practice Range

What are the main issues?

_____

_____

_____

_____

Key approaches/frameworks:

_____

_____

_____

_____

Possible courses of action:

_____

_____

_____

_____

A non-profit in Baltimore runs two separate after-school clubs for children. Although the organization has been in existence for more than a decade and is considered to be an important part of its community, it is suffering financially in a struggling economy and fears that it will soon need to cut services and programs in order to continue operating. What steps should it should consider taking?

Key questions to ask:

_____

_____

_____

What process would you use to investigate this question?

_____

_____

_____

Where would you find the information you need?

_____

_____

The VP of marketing of a successful minor league baseball team would like to attract more kids to the team's games. He has proposed to the team's general manager that kids' tickets be discounted 50 percent for all upcoming season games. Your firm has served the team previously on an unrelated matter, and now the GM is calling you as a trusted advisor to get your point of view before he makes a decision on the kids' marketing plan. What are some of the issues he should consider?

Key questions to ask:

_____

_____

_____

_____

What are the main issues?

_____

_____

_____

_____

Key approaches/frameworks:

_____

_____

_____

_____

Possible courses of action:

_____

_____

_____

_____

Action recommendations:

_____

_____

_____

_____

The Practice Range

Business Strategy Questions

Keep the rules for business strategy questions in mind:

1. Think framework.

2. Ask questions.

3. Work from small to big.

CASE 9

Your client, Rick's Kicks, is a manufacturer of midrange and high-end athletic shoes. The company has been faltering in recent years and is under significant shareholder pressure to grow its business. A major mass merchant has approached the company and expressed interest in launching an offering from your client in all of its stores. (The company currently does not sell to mass merchants.) Should your client go ahead with the launch? If so, how?

Key questions to ask:

_____

_____

_____

_____

What are the main issues?

_____

_____

_____

_____

Key approaches/frameworks:

_____

_____

_____

_____

Outline for my answer:

_____

_____

_____

_____

Action recommendations:

_____

_____

_____

The Practice Range

Your client is a major branded skateboard manufacturer that has decided to enter the Brazilian market. Should it license its brand or manage the entry in-house?

Key questions to ask:

_____

_____

_____

_____

_____

_____

What are the main issues?

_____

_____

_____

_____

_____

_____

Key approaches/frameworks:

_____

_____

_____

_____

Outline for my answer:

_____

_____

_____

_____

Action recommendations:

_____

_____

_____

The Practice Range

Your client is a major car manufacturer with significant sales and brand equity. Though the company is doing well, the CEO is looking for incremental opportunities. A major area of concern is that customers' positive interactions with the brand are largely limited to the car-buying experience, which occurs on average once every three years. How would you increase customers' positive interactions with the brand?

Key questions to ask:

_____

_____

_____

_____

What are the main issues?

_____

_____

_____

_____

_____

Outline for my answer:

Action recommendations:

The Practice Range

WetFeet®

Your firm is involved in a competitive bid with two other consulting firms for a project with a major carbonated soda manufacturer. The company is considering entering the U.S. bottled water market and will be hiring a consulting firm to help it assess the opportunity. The partner leading the proposal effort has asked you to assist her in preparing a presentation for the company's executives. How would you structure the presentation? What issues would you address?

Key questions to ask:

_____

_____

What are the main issues?

_____

_____

Outline for my answer:

_____

_____

_____

Resume Questions

Remember the rules for resume questions:

1. Know your story.

2. Keep the Parent Test in mind.

3. Let your excitement shine!

What would you contribute to the community of our firm outside of your work?

_____

_____

_____

_____

_____

_____

_____

_____

_____

_____

_____

_____

_____

_____

_____

How would your last supervisor describe you if I called for a reference? What would he or she say about your performance? What might he or she say you could have done better?

I see you used to work in product management at the Lee Jeans division of VF Corporation. Describe for me how your product was positioned in the marketplace. What would you say is the biggest challenge facing the Lee brand in the next five years? If you were the CEO, what would you to do meet that challenge?

_____

_____

_____

_____

_____

_____

_____

_____

_____

_____

_____

Nailing the Case

- The Answers

- Market-Sizing Questions

- Business Operations Questions

- Business Strategy Questions

- Resume Questions

The Answers

Now it's time to walk through sample answers to each of the questions given in the previous section. Although we believe that our recommended answers are good, we know that there are many equally good and even better answers out there. Remember, the destination is often less important to your interviewer than the road you take to get there. With that in mind, smooth sailing! A quick note on the layout: Each question is followed by bad answers (which are admittedly a bit far-fetched in some cases) and a good answer. The questions and dialogue between the hypothetical recruiter and candidate appear in normal type; the WetFeet analysis and commentary appear in italics.

Market-Sizing Questions

Case 1

How many golf carts are there in the United States?

This is a straightforward market-sizing question, which would be appropriate for undergraduates and advanced-degree candidates.

Bad Answers

- Too many. Golf is boring, and people who are too lazy to walk really bum me out. Mark Twain said that "golf is a good walk spoiled." He didn't say anything about carts, did he?
  As a general rule of thumb, you'll want to avoid making comments that could offend your interviewer. And while your interviewer may appreciate what you believe to be the erudition of your Twain reference, it's best to answer the question you're asked.

- Let me think through the drivers of that one. Hopefully I can iron it out. Are we out of the woods yet?
  Nice puns. Not funny. Save the jokes for amateur night at the local stand-up comedy club.

Good Answer

Candidate: There are a couple ways of going about answering this question. One way would be to tackle it from the supply side, estimating the production of the major manufacturers and their market shares. The other way would be to approach it from the demand side, taking into account the different uses of golf carts and then estimating how many are employed in each way. I'm going to take the latter approach, given that I have some familiarity with golf that should come in handy.

Good start. The candidate has successfully laid out two high level ways of approaching the problem, and has created a logical structure to use in walking the interviewer through the answer.

Candidate: To begin, I'm going to say that there are two major "buckets" of golf carts-those used on golf courses, and "all other." The second would include things like carts used for maintenance purposes and at retirement communities.

Great job. The candidate is developing the structure and has scored a victory by identifying the "all other" bucket of golf carts. Remember to approach these market-sizing questions with an open mind and to consider all possibilities; the interviewer is testing your ability to think creatively and expansively. Most people would immediately think of only golf carts

used at golf courses and then move on. Make sure to take a second when you begin these market-sizing questions to check that you're thinking broadly (while keeping in mind that you've only got limited time, and you can't turn over every stone).

Candidate: Let's dive into the golf course bucket first. I'm going to generate an estimate for that market, and then come back to the "all other" bucket. This part of the question could be tackled in a few different ways. I'm going to try to estimate the number of golf courses in the country and go from there. Let me start in my own backyard. In San Francisco proper, I'm guessing that there are about 20 golf courses. I know that there are about 800,000 residents of San Francisco, so this equates to one golf course per 40,000 people in San Francisco. For the sake of simplicity, I'm going to assume that this ratio is applicable nationwide. In reality there would be a range, but for the sake of this question, let's assume an average.

The candidate has acknowledged that there are multiple ways of tackling this part of the question, but has put a stake in the ground and is moving forward. The candidate has also grounded the answer in a familiar subject. There's nothing wrong with going about it this way. Just be careful that at the outset of the question you don't use familiarity as a substitute for a structured approach to solving the problem. Finally, the candidate follows the first and second rules of market-sizing questions: use round numbers, and show your work.

Candidate: So, if there's one golf course per 40,000 people in the United States and about 280 million people in the country, that would imply a total of 7,000 golf courses nationwide. As a quick sanity check, that would imply that there are about 150 golf courses per state, which seems reasonable to me. Of course, big states like California will have more while states like North Dakota may have less, but as an average it seems reasonable.

It's always good to triangulate around a number like the candidate is doing here. In addition to beating the term "sanity check" to death on a daily basis, consultants do use

little tools like this one all the time to quickly assess the credibility of an analysis. And while getting to the "right" number is not the point of these kinds of questions, making sure your answer is logical is important.

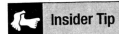
Candidate: Now that I've determined that there are about 7,000 courses in the United States, I need to figure out how many golf carts are at each course. To begin, I know that the average golf course opens at about 7:00 a.m., and lets the last group of players tee off at about 5:00 p.m. Groups of golfers can tee off in about ten minute intervals, which means that between 7:00 a.m. and 5:00 p.m. 60 groups of golfers can tee off (10 hours X 6 groups per hour). I also know that the average round of golf takes about four hours to complete. This means that the same set of golf carts can be used about three times throughout the day. So that means that each of the 20 groups of golfers needs a "unique set" of carts. Since golf carts hold two people, and the average group is a foursome, this means that a golf course would need about 40 carts to meet maximum demand.

Whew! That was a lot of numbers. In a case like this, you should definitely follow the third rule of market-sizing questions and use scratch paper and a calculator if you feel it will help you stay organized. You want to avoid confusing yourself or forgetting numbers.

Candidate: Now I know that there are 7,000 courses in the United States, each of which owns about 40 carts. Doing the math, that means that there are about 280,000 golf carts in the United States in the first bucket—those owned by golf courses. Now we need to move on to the second bucket—the "all other" category.

The candidate has come up with an answer and clearly stated the supporting logic. In addition, the candidate has recalled that this exercise really only solved half of the problem in the way it was initially structured.

Interviewer: That's all right—let's cut it off there so we can move on to some other things. You've done a great job so far, and I'm confident you'd handle the second half of the question well. Nicely done.

Excellent! The interviewer has expressed enough confidence in the candidate's abilities to move on to the next part of the interview.

Case 2

How long does it take a Starbucks to serve enough coffee to completely fill the gas tank of a Hummer?

This is a case designed to test your ability with numbers and your comfort with estimates and assumptions.

Bad Answers

- Great. I'm extremely into the idea of alternative fuels. In fact, I think that SUVs are doing a huge disservice to our environment. It's not like anyone really uses them for off-road driving anyway.
  Be careful about sounding off on social issues unless the conversation is clearly headed that way and the interviewer seems interested in hearing your views. Certainly you should feel comfortable expressing your points of view, but it just may be that your interviewer may drive an SUV, and an answer like this could land you in hot water.

- Ummm, I'd say about two or three hours.
  On a market-sizing question, it's never a good idea to throw out a number without first establishing a framework for thinking about the question and making smart assumptions. Even if you're asked a question that you actually know the answer to (e.g. you work for an electronics company and you're asked how many DVD players are sold in a year), you still want to lay out a structured approach.

Good Answer

Candidate: There are really three components to this question that I'll need to walk through to reach a solution. First, how big is the average cup of coffee sold at an average Starbucks? Second, what is the rate at which Starbucks coffee

is served? And third, how big is the gas tank of a Hummer? Along the way I'll need to do some conversions and some simple arithmetic.

Excellent start. The candidate has clearly laid out an approach for the interviewer and has created a structure to ensure that he stays on track as he moves through the solution.

Candidate: From my own visits to Starbucks, I know that there are a few different sizes available. You can buy a small, a medium, a large, and maybe even a "grande." In any event, let's assume for this question that the average size of a cup of coffee sold is about a pint, which I believe is 16 ounces of coffee.

When the question is open-ended, there's nothing wrong with making an informed assumption about a component part and moving on. Don't get tangled up in too many trivial details. And, as always with market-sizing questions, use round numbers.

Candidate: The question of the rate is a little bit trickier, as that varies depending on the time of day, day of the week, possibly temperature, and even time of the year. To keep things manageable, let's assume that we're talking about a Starbucks that's open five days a week, like the one near my office. The busiest time of day is likely to be the morning rush, between the hours of approximately 7:00 a.m. and 9:00 a.m. At those times, the Starbucks should be staffed most heavily and drawing the greatest crowd, so the rate of service will be higher. At other times of the day, the rate is likely to be slower. So, let's assume that between 7:00 a.m. and 9:00 a.m., two customers per minute are served, and at all other hours of the day, only one customer per minute is served. Therefore, on a weighted average basis, 1.2 customers per minute are served on average throughout the course of the day.

The candidate has handled the somewhat tricky rate question well, first by choosing manageable but believable numbers, and next by displaying his understanding of the concept of weighted averages, a simple but common formula that surfaces all the time in

the world of consulting. In this case, the formula would be: [(2 customers per minute X 2 hours) + (1 customer per minute X 8 hours)] / (10 hours, or 600 minutes) = 1.2 customers per minute.

Candidate: So, 1.2 customers per minute equals 72 customers per hour. And we've already established that each customer on average purchases 16 ounces of coffee. Therefore, in a given hour, there are 72 X 16, or 1,152 ounces of coffee sold. At this point, I need to ask one quick question: I believe that there are 8 pints, or 128 ounces to a gallon. Is that correct?

It's always better to ask the question than to be shy and head down the wrong path. The interviewer will let you know if it's a question you should sort out on your own.

Interviewer: Yes, that's correct. There are 128 ounces to a gallon.

Candidate: Since there are 128 ounces of coffee in a gallon, and 1,152 ounces of coffee sold per hour at Starbucks, that means that there are 9 gallons of coffee purchased each hour. Lastly, assuming that the Hummer has a tank much bigger than the average car, a tank that holds say 45 gallons of gasoline, it would take a Starbucks five hours to sell enough coffee to fill the tank.

Having navigated all of the somewhat tricky parts of the case, the candidate wraps up succinctly and confidently.

Interviewer: Well done.

Case 3

Having fallen on hard times, your consulting firm has decided to serve a notorious bank robber. He has asked you to determine how many briefcases he must bring with him in order to steal $10 million in cash, all $100 bills, in bundles of 1,000 bills each.

This is a market-sizing question in the sense that its purpose is to check your ability to structure your answer and run simple numbers.

Bad Answers

- Your firm works for a bank robber? That sounds so interesting!
  Try to suspend disbelief for a minute here. And no, you'll never do anything as exciting as working for a bank robber—trust us.

- Is the briefcase snakeskin, eel skin, or steel? Based on my limited experience with armed robbery, I'd recommend steel for durability and style.
  As a potential consultant, industry expertise can certainly come in handy on a project. But if that expertise happens to fall in the crime underworld, you may want to hold off on breaking out that piece of information.

Good Answer

Candidate: Well, I can't claim to be terribly familiar with the world of bank robbery, but I can make some good assumptions about the sizes of money and briefcases, and that should be plenty to go on. There are four pieces of information I'll need to crack this case: first, how much cash is in each bundle; second, how many bundles make $10 million; third, what are the dimensions of each bundle; and fourth, what are the dimensions of each briefcase. I plan to move through each of those in order. If it's all right, I'm going to use a bit of scratch paper to keep track of my work-there are lots of numbers in play here.

Nicely done. The candidate has laid out a clear and concise structure for solving the case and has communicated it well to the interviewer. The candidate is well-positioned to attack the problem. You should never be shy about using scratch paper or a calculator if you think you'll need it.

Candidate: All right, let's start with the first piece. This is straightforward enough. I've already been told that each bundle contains one thousand $100 bills. Therefore, multiplying 1,000 by 100 tells me that there is $100,000 in each bundle of cash. To solve the second piece, I simply need to divide $10,000,000

by $100,000 to determine how many bundles my client plans to steal. Canceling out the zeros, I get 100. So, the client will steal 100 bundles of cash to get to his $10 million total. That's the easy part. Now let's move on to determining the size of each bundle and each briefcase.

The candidate is on the right track. He is moving comfortably and smoothly through the arithmetic, using round numbers, and keeping the interviewer well-informed of his thought process.

Candidate: Now on to the size of each bundle. This part is a bit tougher. Initially, when I thought of 1,000 bills stacked atop one another, I imagined the stack would be quite high. But, the more I think about it, the more it seems that the stack wouldn't in fact be that tall. After all, each bill is quite thin, and when bundled together, I imagine they can be compressed rather tightly. In fact, I can remember working at a cash register at a restaurant in high school and unbundling $100 stacks of $1 bills. Each of those was much less than an inch high, even less than half an inch. So if a stack of 100 $1 bills is one-third of an inch high, then a stack of 1,000—ten times as many—will be about 3 inches tall. So that takes care of the height. In addition, I'm going to assume that a bill is—well, in fact, why don't I just take a look at one in my wallet—6 inches long and 2 inches wide.

Here, the candidate draws nicely on personal experience to inform his estimates. Of course, it's a bit contrived on our part, but it's meant to illustrate a point: Wherever possible, rely on fact to substantiate your claims, and be creative when you have to. No one will expect you to "know" how high a stack of 1,000 bills is, but an interviewer will expect you to be creative and structured in how you get to an answer. In addition, the candidate decided to reach into his wallet to get a better read on a piece of information he needed. Be resourceful—especially when you're literally sitting on a piece of data!

Candidate: Next, the size of a briefcase. Briefcases obviously vary in size, but I'm going to take an average. Thinking about my own briefcase, it's certainly big enough to hold a laptop, some notebooks, and other small items. So let's say it's about 18 inches wide, about 12 inches high, and has a depth of about 6 inches. I'm just going to quickly sketch that on my paper to make it easier to visualize. I'm also going to sketch a bundle of money with its associated dimensions.

If it helps you to think visually by drawing things out, do so. There are many cases where diagrams and tables can come in handy, so by all means use them. In addition, notice that the candidate has been smart about using round numbers for the size of the briefcase. In a world where you're making informed assumptions anyway, at least make the math manageable.

Candidate: Now, I just need to arrange the money and figure out how many bundles fit into one briefcase. Picture the briefcase laying flat on a table, with the lid open. I'd start by laying each stack flat on the bottom, oriented vertically. Since the briefcase is 18 inches wide, and each stack of bills is 2 inches high, I can fit nine stacks of bills across the briefcase. And, since each stack is 6 inches wide, I can fit two rows of nine stacks of bills on the bottom of the briefcase. That makes 18 snugly fit bundles on the bottom of the briefcase. In addition, since the stacks are 3 inches high and the briefcase is 6 inches deep, I can double stack the bundles, meaning that I can fit a total of 36 bundles into a single briefcase. Thinking back to the original question, then, if 36 bundles can be stashed in one briefcase, my client will need three briefcases to carry off the $10 million.

Occasionally, candidates will get deep into the piece of a problem they are attempting to solve and forget to take the last small steps necessary to solve the original question. For example, some candidates might determine that 36 bundles can fit in a single briefcase, and, satisfied that they'd come to that point, announce 36 as their answer. Always remember to keep the original question in mind, as this candidate has done.

Case 4

How many unique horse jockeys ride in races in the United States on an average Saturday?

This is a case in which you may need to ask a question or two depending on your familiarity with horse racing. It's fairly straightforward with only a few potential traps, so don't complicate things unnecessarily. Keep an eye out for tip-off words like "unique." It's probably telling you something.

Bad Answers

- A whole lot. Because let me tell you, the last time I was at the racetrack, I got absolutely killed. Wiped out.
  While racetracks surely do make a lot of money, you may not want to detail your personal contribution to their balance sheet this early in the game. It's also not really the point of the question.

- I'm not sure this question is entirely fair. I've never ridden a horse, and I've certainly never watched one or bet on one. Can we try something else?
  Unfortunately, you'll have to deal with whatever question you're given, regardless of your prior experience with the topic. If you're not familiar with a topic, ask questions to navigate your way through. Part of the point of these interviews is to assess your problem-solving abilities in unfamiliar subject areas. After all, you're applying to be a consultant.

Good Answer

Candidate: All right, there are a couple of things I'll need to get at to answer this one. I'm not personally familiar with horseracing, but fundamentally, I need to know how many horse racetracks there are in the United States and how many horses run at each one on an average Saturday. Figuring out how many horses run will allow me to determine how many jockeys there are. There will be a couple of complications to deal with—for example, how many races take place in a day at each track, and whether jockeys can ride more than one horse in a day. But I'll deal with those issues in a bit.

Simple but effective start. The candidate acknowledges that he's not an expert in the area, but still confidently establishes a framework for evaluating the question. He also calls out a few potentially tricky points that may arise.

Candidate: Let's begin with the racetrack side of things. I grew up in St. Louis, and though I never went to it, I know there was one racetrack in the area. St. Louis is a medium-sized city, but it's the largest city in Missouri. So I'd imagine there may be one other racetrack in Missouri, possibly in another medium-sized city like Kansas City. So given that, I'd assume that the 25 smallest states may have two racetracks each, and that the 25 largest states may have three to four racetracks each. For example, it seems reasonable that a state like California may have at least one racetrack around each San Francisco, Los Angeles, and San Diego, if not more. Given that, I'm actually going to assume that the five largest states have five racetracks each, the second largest 20 states have three racetracks each, and the smallest 25 states have two racetracks each. So that would make a total of 135 racetracks in the United States. I don't want to get too detailed here, but I'm going to round the number down to 130 to account for the fact that a state like Utah, and maybe a couple of others, may not have any racetracks at all.

The candidate chose to use a market segmentation approach to get to his estimate of the number of racetracks in the United States. He did a good job of thinking out loud without rambling, and revised his estimates on the fly when he realized that the very biggest states could actually have more racetracks than he initially imagined. And he went for some nice bonus points at the end when he assumed that gambling of any kind may be illegal in Utah. Creativity is a good thing in these interviews; just don't go overboard.

Candidate: All right, now I'm going to think about the number of horses at a given racetrack. First, can you tell me how many horses run in an average race? I could guess, but I'm really not familiar with the sport.

Again, it's okay to ask questions when you need more information.

Interviewer: It varies, but on average, and to make the numbers round, you could assume that there are ten horses in a race.

Candidate: Thank you. That's helpful. Now I have another follow-up question. Is there only one race run per day at a track, or are there several?

Good. Although the candidate is not familiar with the topic, he's turning over all the right stones and thoroughly examining the issue.

Interviewer: Good question. In fact, there are almost always several races run per day. On average, there may be about nine races run each day at each track.

The interviewer is readily answering the candidate's questions, indicating that there's no problem with asking them.

Candidate: Great. To sum up where I am so far, there are 130 racetracks in the United States, each of which hosts nine races with ten horses on a Saturday. I'm interested, however, in the number of jockeys, not the number of horses, so there are just a couple more steps I need to take before I can come to an answer.

In a case that is drawn out and potentially a bit confusing, briefly summing up where you are can be a good idea.

Candidate: I'm assuming that while each horse can probably only run one race per day, jockeys may be able to ride in more than one race. Exhaustion and injury are less relevant to jockeys, and they likely want to maximize their potential winnings by running more than one race. So I'm going to guess that a jockey could ride in three races per Saturday. Therefore, the number of *unique* jockeys at each track is 30 (9 races X 10 horses *divided by* 3). That gives an answer of 130 racetracks X 30 jockeys, or 3,900 jockeys per Saturday.

Again, the candidate has done an excellent job of exploring the possible intricacies of a topic that he is admittedly not familiar with. The insight about jockeys riding more than one race per day is an important one. Remember, you were given a hint to this part of the answer with the word "unique" in the question.

Interviewer: Is there anything you've forgotten? Will every track be open on a given Saturday?

The candidate believes he's finished the question, but the interviewer is probing a bit further, possibly to see how the candidate will respond to a bit of pressure. Stay calm—your ability to deliver under a bit of pressure will obviously be key to your success as a consultant.

Candidate: Good question. You're right; I didn't initially think of that. My answer is likely valid for a spring or summer day, when the weather is warm and all racetracks are probably open. But in the winter, many of the racetracks in the Northeast, Midwest, and other cold and snowy parts of the country could be closed. So on a Saturday in the winter or the fall, the number of jockeys may be about 2,000, or approximately half as many. And on a weighted average Saturday, the number would be 3,000, or about halfway between.

The candidate maintained his poise, caught on to the gist of the interviewer's question, and delivered a solid answer.

Interviewer: Nice job. Not bad for someone who's never been to the races. Let's move on to the next question.

Case 5

The general manager of a popular ski resort has called on you to help her figure out why her resort has been experiencing declining profits over the past three years. How would you help her?

This is a commonly asked case question about the potential reasons for and responses to a drop in profits. You'll encounter questions like these referring to various industries, but the approach to solving them is similar.

Bad Answer

Candidate: Well, it's got to be the lack of powder in recent years. Ski resorts are totally dependent on getting good snow, unless they can make their own, but no one likes to ski the artificial stuff as much anyway. And I know that the last few years have been really tough for snow. So, tough as it is, the manager needs to hold out hope that the next few years will be better ones.

Yikes! Slow down. Poor snowfall could certainly be a part of the problem, but has the candidate really asked enough questions to know the answer?

Interviewer: Actually, snowfall in the part of the country this resort is in has been consistent in recent years, and the ski season has been no shorter than normal. So that's not the root cause. What else could be going on here? How else could you structure the problem to get to the answer?

The candidate has been thrown a lifeline.

Candidate: Okay. If it's not the snow, then it's got to be the prices. The last time I went skiing it cost me almost $100 for the day with the lift ticket and food. Not to mention beers at the end of the day. With prices that high, who can afford to go?

The candidate has ignored the lifeline and decided to swim for it. Unfortunately, he's sinking quickly, as he has failed to generate any kind of structure and continues to take wild, unsubstantiated guesses at the answer.

Good Answer

Candidate: If profits are down, then either costs are up, revenues are down, or both. Have costs increased in recent years?

The candidate has successfully recognized this as a profit question, and has introduced the profit equation.

Interviewer: Actually, no. Assuming that I'm the client, I can tell you that costs have even declined a bit in recent years as we've improved sourcing in our food operations and decreased snowmaking.

So it's not costs—carry on.

Candidate: Okay, so if the problem is not fundamentally on the cost side, it must be on the revenue side. Has visitation to the mountain decreased, or have prices decreased?

Clearly, then, since we're not dealing with a cost issue, it's a revenue problem. The candidate has identified price and volume as the component parts of revenue.

Interviewer: Prices have not dropped; in fact, they've increased slightly with inflation. The number of visitors to the mountain has decreased, though.

Candidate: All right. Now, what's happening in the industry at large? Are other ski resorts experiencing similar declines? If so, are their declines in profit in line with those at your resort?

The candidate has wisely turned to understanding the current dynamics of the industry. Doing so will allow her to determine whether she's dealing with a market share or a market-size problem.

Interviewer: Yes, other resorts are struggling as well. At a recent trade show I spoke with executives from dozens of other resorts, and they're all experiencing the same things that I am. Visitor numbers and profits are down.

The candidate continues to make good progress through her framework and has identified the forces at work in creating the profit problem. Now she'll need to dive deeper.

Candidate: Right. So we've determined that customers are leaving, and they're not migrating to other ski mountains, since everyone is struggling. I want to dig deeper into who exactly is leaving so we can develop some hypotheses around why they might be doing so. Are there certain types of customers who are leaving in greater numbers than others? For example, customers of a certain age or background or geographic location?

Given that there is an industrywide visitation decline in place, the candidate has decided to pursue a customer segmentation path to see what it reveals. A completely random migration of customers would present a set of issues much different than a migration among a specific consumer segment.

Interviewer: Hmmm. Unfortunately, I'm really not sure. We don't do as good of a job as we should of tracking our customers' profiles. So I'm afraid I can't tell you that.

Situations in which data is limited and/or difficult to access are extremely common to consulting projects. As a consultant, you'll often be called upon to make smart assumptions and take creative approaches to difficult problems.

Candidate: Let's try a slightly different approach. I know that you sell a range of different ski tickets, everything from season passes down to half-day tickets. In addition, I imagine you also generate revenue from concessions and equipment rentals? Can you tell me how the revenue decline has broken out along those lines?

The candidate has wisely decided to pursue a slightly different line of questioning, but one that may still lead her to some kind of segmentation and/or valuable information concerning the specifics of the revenue decline.

Interviewer: That I can help you with. Our food business has declined, but no faster or slower than our visitation rate. Basically, each skier purchases an average amount of food and beverages, and those businesses have declined linearly with visitation. Tickets and rentals, however, are a different story. Revenues from rentals have declined twice as fast as visitation, and our sales of half-day and full-day lift passes have dropped more precipitously than our sales of full-week tickets and season passes.

Now we're getting somewhere! The candidate's persistence has paid off—clearly something is driving the disproportionate decline in the rental and short-duration lift ticket businesses.

Candidate: Great. That's extremely helpful. My hypothesis is that less-experienced skiers are not coming to the mountain as frequently. I believe this because both rentals and shorter-term lift ticket sales are down; I would think that these products are purchased most often by beginning skiers. More experienced skiers are more likely to own their equipment, and therefore less

likely to rent, and are also far more likely to purchase a season pass. Do those assumptions seem reasonable?

The candidate has formed a fact-based hypothesis, and has "sanity-checked" it with the interviewer. Always keep in mind that the interviewer (who, in this case, is playing the role of the client) is an expert in the industry, so be sure to approach problems confidently but not arrogantly.

Interviewer: Yes, I think you're on to something. Those assumptions do seem reasonable, and now that you mention it, it reminds me that our revenue from ski lessons is way down as well. And those services are used most by beginning skiers. So let's assume that we're right, and that beginners aren't showing up as often. What are some ways you might go about fixing it?

The candidate has gotten to the bottom of the "why" behind the revenue decline—less experienced skiers are no longer coming to the mountain as often as they used to. The interviewer has decided to probe a bit around the "how"—that is, what can be done to fix the problem and restore profits.

Candidate: A few of the areas I'd begin to think about are marketing, pricing, and getting a better understanding of who that beginning consumer is and why he or she may be leaving. First, on the marketing front, how is your resort being promoted? I'm a fairly experienced skier, and I know that a lot of the advertising I see contains images of people skiing through deep powder and jumping off of cliffs. Maybe that kind of imagery is a turn-off to beginners, who may be more scared than inspired by it. So a safer, less intimidating marketing approach could be more comforting to this consumer segment. I've also noticed that certain ski resorts have been experimenting with slow-skiing "family ski areas" on the mountain. That may be something to try.

Second, skiing is certainly an expensive sport, and while I wouldn't recommend a price decrease in an environment of falling profits—especially without more

data-maybe we could explore some more creative pricing arrangements. For example, what about bundling free lessons with a lift ticket for first-time skiers? An offer like that could attract a reluctant first-timer to give skiing a try.

And third, in terms of understanding the consumer, I'd certainly want to develop some ways to collect more data on the people who are visiting your mountain. I'd also hypothesize that there are a lot of activities these days that are competing for consumers' disposable dollars. With the explosion of all kinds of outdoor sports, customers who aren't already hooked on skiing may be sampling a host of other sports, and you are probably competing for a share of their wallets as much as anything else.

The candidate has certainly risen to the interviewer's challenge by laying out a clear framework and proposing a host of creative ideas for action. Would you be expected to come up with a list this comprehensive in a live interview? Not necessarily, and this candidate is obviously familiar enough with skiing to generate a detailed list of suggestions. But when you're asked for potential practical solutions to a problem, be fact-based, rely on what you've learned in the case so far, and be creative.

Interviewer: That's a great list. We've got a lot of work ahead of us, but I'm confident that we're on the right track.

Case 6

Your client is a publisher of romance novels that sells to retail bookstores. The standard arrangement in the industry is that publishers must reimburse their customers at the end of the year for any unsold inventory. In this case, you are to assume that any inventory that is sent back to the publisher must be destroyed, and has no resale value. One of your client's customers has made a proposal: for a 10 percent discount on wholesale prices, they will no longer send back any books at the end of the year.

Should the publisher do the deal? The following data exists:

- In 2002, the client sold 10,000 books to the bookstore.

- Client's production facilities are partially self-owned domestically, and partially contracted to overseas vendors, primarily in Asia.

- The average wholesale price of a book in 2002 was $10.

- It costs the client $5 on average to make a single book.

- The romance novel segment of the publishing industry has been flat for almost a decade, and is expected to remain so in coming years.

- In 2002, the bookstore sent back 20 percent of its order to the client at the end of the year.

It's not uncommon for consulting firms to be hired to evaluate deals of various kinds, including mergers, acquisitions, and partnerships. This case is designed to evaluate your capacity to weigh the various dimensions of a deal and make a recommendation.

Bad Answer

Candidate: I'd recommend destroying the romance novels before they even hit the shelves in the first place. Nonetheless, the answer seems simple enough to arrive at—we'll just figure out which way the client is likely to make more money, and we'll go with that one.

The candidate actually raises one of the key dimensions of the case—relative profitability—albeit in a blunt and borderline offensive way.

Interviewer: Okay. The more profitable option will certainly be important. But is there anything else you might consider structurally before we dive in?

The interviewer has looked past some of the less-appealing parts of the candidate's answer and is probing for more information and a framework.

Candidate: Honestly, I used to be an M&A banker, and the deals were all about the bottom line. I don't see how this would be any different. So let's just dive into the numbers and see how it shakes out.

Apparently consulting isn't the field for this guy. The candidate has stubbornly refused to follow the interviewer's lead, and continues to see the problem in one-dimensional terms.

Good Answer

Candidate: Interesting question. To approach it, I think I first need to determine the relative economics of the present scenario versus the proposed scenario. Then we can delve into some of the related issues around things like supply chain and retail relationship that may arise depending on how the numbers look. To begin with, I need to understand the publisher's profitability on the bookstore's account in the present time. To do so, let's first tackle revenues, and then costs.

The candidate has clearly identified her proposed approach to the problem, acknowledging that the economics must be resolved first, followed by any ancillary issues that may surface depending upon which scenario proves more attractive financially.

Candidate: First, revenue. I know from the data given that the client sold 10,000 books to this customer last year, at a price of $10 per book. Therefore, its gross revenue on the account was $100,000 in 2002. However, I also know that the same bookstore returned 20 percent of its initial order at the end of the year for a full refund. Therefore, the store's returned 2,000 books for a $20,000 refund, bringing the net revenue to $80,000.

The candidate has moved swiftly and clearly through the revenue side of the current scenario, keeping in mind the issue of the returned books and its impact on the client's revenue line.

Candidate: Now on to the cost piece, which is pretty straightforward. I know that the fixed cost per book is $5, bringing the client's total cost to produce the books for the customer to $50,000. Unfortunately, the books that the customer returned represent sunk costs for the client. Since the only option is to destroy

the books, and since the store is due a full refund, there's nothing the client can do to recover its costs on those 2,000 returned books.

The candidate has demonstrated her command of the data, and her understanding of the issues around the client's return/refund arrangement with the bookstore.

Candidate: Therefore, since the client generated $80,000 in net revenue, and spent $50,000 to do so, the client collected a profit of $30,000 from the account in 2002. So now let's take a look at estimated revenues under the scenario that the bookstore has proposed. Under the terms of the deal, the client would no longer be responsible for any unsold inventory. But the client would also need to provide a 10 percent discount, bringing wholesale prices down to $9. To complete the revenue picture under the new scenario, I need to know how many books the client could expect to sell over a year period. Is there data on that point?

The candidate has moved on to evaluating the proposed deal and is taking the same approach to the problem as she did for the previous part.

Interviewer: That work is currently under way. What do you think?

The interviewer obviously doesn't want to give that piece of information away just yet; he wants to test the candidate's judgment on the issue.

Candidate: Let me think about it in the context of last year's sales. Since the bookstore won't be at liberty to return any books in the proposed scenario, it's likely to order less than it initially did in 2002. I already know that the market for romance novels is expected to remain flat, so there's no reason to believe that the store will sell more books next year than it did in 2002. So I'd imagine that this customer will order at most 8,000 books, which is the amount it sold in 2002. However, since the bookstore will be bearing all the risk in the new scenario, it may be likely to hedge a bit and buy less than it sold in 2002. So let's assume that it will buy 7,500 books in the new scenario. Does that seem

reasonable? And additionally, would the cost of producing books change for the client if it were manufacturing only 7,500 books?

The candidate has done three things well here. First, she has drawn on the data given about market dynamics to hypothesize that the store's sales are likely to be flat next year. Second, she has kept a possible fluctuation in cost in mind. And third, she has articulated a key shift in the relationship dynamic that would occur under the proposed scenario-that is, the shift in which party bears the risk.

Interviewer: In fact, 7,500 books is exactly where we've come out in our initial analysis as well. So let's go with 7,500 for now. And to your second question, the cost of production would remain $5.

Nice coincidence! The candidate is right on track, which is always a good thing.

Candidate: Great. Therefore, in the new scenario, the client would generate $67,500 in revenue ($9 x 7,500 books), at a cost of $37,500 ($5 x 7,500 books), resulting in a profit of $30,000. Well, that's interesting. It seems that the client's profitability in both scenarios would be the same. I have to admit I wasn't expecting that.

Surprise, surprise. The numbers have magically worked out to produce economically equivalent scenarios. So now the question gets interesting.

Interviewer: The same, eh? Hmm. So, what should the client do?

It's the moment of truth. The candidate was expecting the numbers to reveal the answer, but they've actually just raised another question. Time for her to think on her feet.

Candidate: I need a bit more information first. Can you tell me how long it takes for the client to fulfill an order? The reason I ask is I want to understand how long it would take the client to replenish the bookstore's supply in the event that all of the client's books sold out.

The candidate is now starting to probe around the related issues she referred to at the beginning of the case. She is wisely being deliberate about collecting a bit more information before making a recommendation.

Interviewer: On average, it takes the client about four weeks from the time of an order to produce a book and get it on-shelf.

Candidate: Given what I know, my recommendation would be for the client to reject the proposal for four reasons. First, given that it takes four weeks for a newly ordered book to hit the shelves, the client could lose valuable sales and shelf space in the event that the bookstore sells out of its initial stock. Second, the client should be nervous about the incentive it would create in the new scenario. That is, I think it's dangerous to create a situation in which your customer is incentivized financially to buy less from you. Third, I imagine that entering into this arrangement with this customer could create issues with the client's other accounts. In some industries, wholesale price differentials are not technically legal and require complicated maneuvering to accomplish. And lastly, the client is in a more advantageous cash flow position in its current situation. It's taking in $100,000 at the beginning of the year, versus an estimated $67,500 in the new scenario. The client has to be prudent about having a cash reserve on hand to pay out any potential returns at the end of the year, but it can certainly put that additional cash to work in the interim.

On the other hand, one could rightfully suggest that destroying the returned books is wasteful, and that in the new scenario that waste may be avoided. While I acknowledge the logic in that argument, I believe it is outweighed by the factors in favor of the current scenario.

The candidate has laid out a cogent, fact-based case to support her recommendation. She has also briefly considered the opposing argument to anticipate potential pushback.

Interviewer: Well done.

Case 7

A non-profit in Baltimore runs two separate after-school clubs for children. Although the organization has been in existence for more than a decade and is considered to be an important part of its community, it is suffering financially in a struggling economy and fears that it will soon need to cut services and programs in order to continue operating. What steps should it should consider taking?

This is a turnaround question embedded in a non-profit context. More and more consulting firms are serving non-profit organizations, and there is a good chance that you will end up consulting on a non-profit project. While many of the issues these organizations face are similar to those encountered by for-profit corporations, remember to be attuned to areas that may be unique to non-profits.

Bad Answers

- I've obviously done a lot of volunteer work in my day. Just read my business school essays. But I didn't sign up for consulting to serve non-profits. Bring on the meaty strategy work.
  This answer won't cut it. Consulting firms serve many non-profits, and the work is taken just as seriously as work for for-profit operations.

- Even in a struggling economy, there are plenty of people out there with cash to donate to organizations like this one. Consider my buddy. He founded a software company focused on optimizing distribution networks for wholesalers of pet birds, and now he's retired and totally loaded. But no one has called him to ask for money. So I'm sure a better fundraising and development strategy would fix these guys up.
  Obviously, no one cares about this guy's buddy. Especially the interviewer. While the candidate has hit upon one potential area of concern—fundraising—he's done so in a wholly speculative and totally crass way.

Good Answer

Candidate: Interesting case, and definitely a fulfilling project to be a part of, I'd imagine. Although this is a case about a non-profit, I think that many of the

same principles I'd bring to bear in a for-profit engagement will come into play here. To begin, I'm going to think about revenues and costs, revenues in the case of a non-profit being fundraising and grant dollars. Have revenues been down recently?

The candidate has taken a logical, though simple, approach. Now on to isolating the main issue!

Interviewer: Revenues, as you call them, have been down, but they've been down for just about everybody in the non-profit sector. In addition, the after-school clubs each have truly best-in-class development directors on staff, and you're not going to add much value here as a consultant.

Ouch. Obviously not the right path. The interviewer is slightly prickly and is sending a pretty strong signal that he doesn't believe that revenues are the issue. You'll have to use your judgment in a situation like this: Is the interviewer really trying to steer you away from a given line of inquiry, or is he testing your persistence and your willingness to push on in the face of resistance?

Candidate: Okay. Revenues aren't the issue here. Let's move on to the cost side then. You mentioned that this organization has been operating for a decade, so it seems that it has fallen on hard times only recently. Have costs increased in recent years? For example, has headcount or average salary increased, or have rental rates been on the rise?

The candidate has decided to backpedal away from the revenue issue and has moved on to the cost side.

Interviewer: Not really. Costs as a percentage of revenue have remained constant for pretty much the entire period the organization has been in operation. To be honest, you're really not getting at the core issues here. Would you maybe like to know some of the basic facts surrounding the organization?

Yikes. The interviewer remains pretty tough and is communicating very clearly that he thinks that the candidate is off-track. Remember, there is obviously an element of role-play at work here, so don't freak out if you meet a tough interviewer. Clients can be tough too, and the interviewer is likely testing your reaction to difficult situations.

Candidate: Okay, let's back up a bit then. It seems that I jumped in a bit too fast. I think I need to learn a bit more about the organization, what it does, how it's structured, and the students it serves.

The candidate has calmly acknowledged that he may have leaped in too quickly and is trying out a different course.

Interviewer: Well, as I mentioned at the outset, the organization runs two separate after-school clubs. It owns each of its facilities, both of which are in different parts of downtown Baltimore. Each club serves about 200 unique students, and offers a variety of programs, including sports, arts, woodworking, and tutoring. There is some overlap in the programs offered at each facility, but they aren't identical. For example, one facility offers computer-training classes, and the other doesn't. Each facility has a staff of about 25.

Good. The interviewer seems to have mellowed out a bit and given out a bit of useful information.

Candidate: Okay, that's helpful. I want to probe a bit more on the organizational side of things. You mentioned that each club employs about 25 people, and earlier you alluded to the fact that each club has its own director of development. Is there a central or headquarters office? What functions are shared between the two clubs?

The candidate has detected that this case has an organizational element to it and has decided to explore that route a bit. The candidate also smartly remembered part of the answer to the question he asked earlier about revenues. Even though his initial path

may have been the wrong one, he rightly sensed that there may have been some useful information in the answer to one of his questions.

Interviewer: There is no central "office" per se, because there never really needed to be. There is an executive director who is the organization's leader, but she uses office space in one of the two facilities. The director of each facility reports into the executive director. Why do you ask?

The interviewer didn't divulge much here, but the "why do you ask" at the end may indicate that the candidate is getting warmer.

Candidate: The reason I'm asking is that I'm wondering whether there isn't some leverage that the organization could gain that it's not currently benefiting from. For example, why is it necessary for each club to have its own development director for fundraising? Is that a function that could potentially be centralized? Certainly each club needs its own staff of counselors, tutors, and so on to work with the kids. But it would seem that some of the more "corporate roles" could be shared. Is this something that's been explored?

The candidate continues to push on an area that seems promising to him.

Interviewer: It's funny you ask that. The client explored centralizing some of its functions a few years back, but eventually decided not to. The executive director was initially interested in the idea, but she was ultimately convinced to keep things as is by the facility directors. So each facility maintains a staff of people who work with the students, as well as development, marketing, membership, and administrative staff.

The interviewer continues to dish out subtle but helpful hints. It seems we're finally getting somewhere.

Candidate: That's interesting. Given the kind of difficulty this client is facing at the moment, I think that the centralization option needs to be seriously

considered again. This may be presumptuous, but one could easily see why the facility directors could have a vested interest in keeping the operation decentralized. After all, it has employees to protect, and would presumably prefer to keep as much of its operations as possible under their own control. So there's certainly a chance that their advice to continue operating "as is" was based on some strong personal biases. In addition, a few years ago, when the client last considered the possibility of centralization, the economy was quite a bit stronger, and it could probably afford to maintain separate operations. The context has certainly shifted since then.

The candidate has become comfortable that he has reached a point where he can start putting some hypotheses out there. Consulting firms obviously take on a lot of cost-focused cases that sometimes result in headcount reduction, especially in tough economic times. Nonetheless, if you're confronted by a case like this, approach the issues with sensitivity and tact.

Interviewer: Okay. What specifically do you mean by centralization here?

Candidate: I guess I'd actually consider something a bit beyond centralization. In fact, somewhat of a merger, if you could call it that, could be in order. It seems clear to me that functions like development, marketing, and membership could be consolidated for the two facilities. That would allow best practices to be shared across the two facilities and could generate substantial cost savings and scale opportunities. In addition, you mentioned earlier that each club supports a unique group of students. In that way, this sounds like a classic synergy opportunity. The clubs can merge their back-office operations without fear of providing redundant services to overlapping markets.

The candidate has put somewhat of a stake in the ground. Owing to what seems to be the desperate nature of the situation, he believes that bold measures are in order.

Interviewer: What are some of the other issues you might consider in pursuing a merger like this?

Candidate: I'd consider a set of both external and internal issues. Externally, I'd think first about its students, and make sure that a merger of the sort I've proposed wouldn't negatively impact the level of service the organization could provide to them. Given that the consolidation I've suggested is limited to the back office, it seems unlikely that it would impact the students' experiences. I'd also think about donors and grant-givers, and consider whether the merger would negatively affect their perceptions of the organization or their desire to contribute. Internally, I would explore strategic, organizational, operational, and cultural issues. Given their shared missions and unique sets of students, the facilities would seem to be strategically aligned. Are there plans to add more facilities in the future? If so, how would that affect the strategic outlook? Are there cultural differences that would make a merger of the clubs problematic?

Interviewer: That's a good starting list. Nice job—that's a tough case. There's obviously not much data to get your hands around.

Case 8

The VP of marketing of a successful minor league baseball team would like to attract more kids to the team's games. He has proposed to the team's general manager that kids' tickets be discounted 50 percent for all upcoming season games. Your firm has served the team previously on an unrelated matter, and now the GM is calling you as a trusted advisor to get your point of view before he makes a decision on the kids' marketing plan. What are some of the issues he should consider?

This is a deceptively tricky question that can reveal multiple layers of complexity as you get deeper and deeper into it. The way in which the question was posed—that is,

you're on a phone call helping the GM think through some issues—is both a hint and a lifeline. You won't necessarily be expected to come to a concrete or comprehensive answer, but you'll need to be insightful about calling out the issues of concern.

Bad Answer

Candidate: Fifty percent off seems like a pretty hefty discount to offer for kids. Kids love baseball anyway, so why is it necessary to offer them such a big discount? It's the parents who should be getting the discount; after all, they're the ones who have to endure three hours of minor league baseball. I'd axe the discount idea and maintain the current pricing structure. A discount—especially one that steep—just won't pay off.

In addition to being brash and off-putting, the candidate has jumped to some pretty decisive conclusions without gathering any of the information he'd need to make them. The candidate has obliquely raised a couple of issues that may prove to be important—opportunity cost and target audience of the promotion—but not in a way that would be helpful to the GM.

Interviewer: Let's take a step back. It sounds like you believe that a discount may not be necessary on kids' tickets. Why might that be the case?

The interviewer has taken pity on our abrasive candidate and chosen to focus on the one bright spot in his previous answer.

Candidate: I think I said why. I just don't think you need to give money away to fans who already love the game and who probably show up in droves anyway. It's like giving away beers in the bleacher seats.

Whatever bright spot existed has surely now faded into darkness. The interviewer was clearly probing for a more fact-based approach, but the candidate didn't step up to the plate, so to speak.

Good Answer

Candidate: Interesting question, fun topic. Though this question seems pretty straightforward, I can see already where there are several moving parts at work here. I want to focus my advice on the core issues that I believe should really drive the GM's decision on this one. I want to get him thinking about those issues so that he's asking the right questions when he sits down with his VP of marketing to hash this out. To me, those core issues are opportunity cost, total fan profitability, and future fan value. I'll start ticking through those, and I'm sure that questions and related issues will come up as I go.

The candidate has acknowledged the potential complexity of the question, and has also indicated that he has picked up on the hints in the question structure. He plans to take an 80/20 approach, hitting what he believes to be the critical issues at the heart of the question first.

Interviewer: Sounds like a good approach. Jump in.

Candidate: Let's start with opportunity cost. By opportunity cost, I mean what would the team potentially forgo in terms of revenue by offering seats to kids at a 50 percent discount? A host of questions that surface in my mind related to this issue: What does attendance look like over the season at games, in terms of a distribution? We'd need to look at not only average attendance, but also the percentage of games that are sold out, the percentage of games that are sold to 90 percent of capacity, and so on. Looking at the attendance profile in that way would allow the team to begin to understand the potential revenue impact of offering a discount on kids' seats.

Additionally, we'd need to look at how many kids are already attending games. There is a danger that the promotion wouldn't attract new kids but would instead simply attract the same kids at lower prices. That's a scenario we'd clearly want to avoid, and we'd need to look at whatever demographic attendance data is available to get behind that one.

Lastly, I'd want to think about the true target of the discount ticket campaign, because that issue impacts the opportunity-cost analysis. Since kids are unlikely to pay for tickets themselves or to come to the games unaccompanied by a parent, it's not hard to argue that the actual target of the marketing campaign is the parent, and not the child. Given that dynamic, the GM would need to think about whether the team might experience a lift in adult attendance by targeting kid fans. If so, the opportunity cost of the discount campaign could be lower than expected. There are other questions that affect the opportunity cost dynamic, but the ones I've just mentioned represent the starting point for getting at the key issues.

Excellent start. The candidate identified opportunity cost as a critical issue, and raised several important related questions. The candidate also earned some brownie points by calling out the benefit of a distribution versus an average in looking at attendance. The distribution vs. average issue is a common one faced by consultants, as averages can be deceptive and can mask important underlying variations in data.

Interviewer: To go a step further, let's assume for a second that all of the games are sold out to adult fans. Would that be enough information to tell you that the discount promotion is a bad idea?

Candidate: Good question. My answer is "not necessarily." In fact, that question leads directly to my next point about profitability. The cost of admission is only one element of a fan's total spend at a baseball game. Ballparks also generate considerable revenue from food, beverage, and souvenir sales. In this case, it would be important to get an understanding from the GM of how the revenues break out by product-that is, by ticket sales vs. the other categories of items. Furthermore, it would be most important to understand the total profitability of a kid fan vs. other fans. Hypothetically, are kids more profitable because they purchase more souvenirs and more snacks? Or, are adults in fact more profitable because they purchase high-margin products like beer? We can't be sure of

the answers to these questions from the information given, but they would be critical for the GM to understand as he comes to a decision on the VP's proposal. Fundamentally, then, the GM would want to determine whether the non-ticket purchases of a kid fan are substantial enough to offset the cost of a discounted ticket, and make a kid fan at least equally as profitable as an adult. Lastly, much of the potential complexity of this case stems from the need to look at the variables of opportunity cost and profitability simultaneously, and not separately as I have done. While my phone call with the GM wouldn't be the appropriate forum for diving into that issue in depth, I'd certainly plan to make him aware of the need to do so in any detailed analysis.

The candidate smartly sees the trick embedded in the interviewer's question, and in so doing calls attention to his understanding of one of the key nuances of the case. That is, even if all games are sold out to adult fans, it's possible that offering the kids' promotion would increase profits. In addition, the candidate rightly notes one of the complexities of the case-the interaction of the opportunity cost and profitability variables—and handles the issue in a smart way.

Interviewer: I see. So potential lost revenue from discounted tickets isn't the only issue to consider. Interesting. What else?

The candidate continues to make good progress through his framework and has identified the forces at work in creating the profit problem. Now he needs to dig deeper.

Candidate: Lastly, I'd encourage the GM to think a bit about future fan value. I don't think this issue is as crucial as the other two I've raised, but I think it's important to keep in mind. Is there any research the team has done that maps the lifetime attendance patterns of their fans? Is there a benefit to getting kids interested in the team early on? Will doing so make them more loyal fans as they become teenagers and adults? I know from my own experience that I'm still a follower of the teams that my parents introduced me to when I was very young, even though I've since moved to another city. While long-term value

may not be the critical driver in the GM's choice, it may be an important consideration if the economics of the proposed promotion prove to be a toss-up. That is, a future value consideration could serve as an important input if the economics alone don't prove decisive.

The candidate has raised an issue that he believes is interesting but of secondary importance and has specified how he'd think about the issue in the context of the case.

Interviewer: You've done a good job hitting on some of the key issues. Now, imagine that you're at the end of your phone call with the GM. He thanks you for raising such insightful issues, but before hanging up, he wants to get your ideas on alternative kids-oriented promotions the team might offer if he opts against the 50 percent discount. What suggestions would you have?

This is one of those situations in which the interviewer is pushing for "extra credit." The interviewer seems satisfied with the candidate's handling of the case thus far, and this is one of those places where you can really shine as an interviewee who went beyond the call of duty.

Candidate: Sure. First, let's assume that the attendance distribution analysis shows that some games are sold out year after year while others are not. Maybe the team could offer discount kids' tickets to the games that aren't sold out. The VP has proposed that the promotion be in effect at all games, but that's not the only possible model. Second, 50 percent off may not be the magic number. Could 25 percent work? What about 10 percent? Whatever the number, if a discount route was chosen, it would be important to run a variety of scenarios to determine the optimal level. Third, maybe a discount isn't necessary at all. For example, maybe the team could attract kids to the games at full price through creative promotions like "all full-paying kids get to come onto the field three hours before the game," or "all full-paying kids can meet three players before the game." There may be other variables outside of price that would influence a fan's decision to come to a game.

Great job. Extra credit awarded! The candidate put forth a few well-reasoned suggestions without hesitation.

Interviewer: Great. I think the GM will appreciate your input. Maybe he'll even hire you to help him on this one.

Business Strategy Questions

Case 9

Your client, Rick's Kicks, is a manufacturer of midrange and high-end athletic shoes. The company has been faltering in recent years, and is under significant shareholder pressure to grow its business. A major mass merchant has approached the company and expressed interest in launching an offering from your client in all of its stores. (The company currently does not sell to mass merchants.) Should your client go ahead with the launch? If so, how?

This is a common growth strategy question centered on channels of distribution. It is appropriate for all levels of candidates, though MBA candidates should expect to tackle the issues in more detail.

Bad Answers

- Mass merchants can be too big and too demanding to do business with. They're almost as likely to drive Rick's Kicks out of business as they are to improve profitability. A lot of brands have been driven into serious trouble

by mass merchants, given their market power and aggressive discounting. If it were me, I'd focus on growing the brand in current channels of distribution. *While there are certainly some potential pitfalls in doing business with mass merchants, dismissing out of hand the option of selling to the world's largest retailers seems a bit hasty.*

- I'm fully convinced that there's a significant market opportunity with mass merchants. No argument there. It's the brand I'd be primarily concerned about. Nonetheless, if the alternative is letting the business slowly slide away, then I think Rick's Kicks needs to take the leap and see what happens. *The candidate raises two decent points: the size of the mass market and brand risk. But he comes to a conclusion too quickly and doesn't display a nuanced understanding of how Rick's Kicks could confront the brand risk in a thoughtful way.*

Good Answer

Candidate: This is definitely a fascinating question, and one that continues to challenge a lot of brands. Broadly speaking, I see two buckets of issues: the quantitative and the qualitative. Within the first bucket, I'll want to tackle the drivers of Rick's Kicks current performance, channel dynamics in the marketplace, cost issues surrounding a potential mass channel entry, and the competitive landscape. On the qualitative side, if we assume for the moment that Rick's Kicks ultimately enters the mass channel, the fundamental issue to consider is branding as it relates to the existing brand, a potential new brand launch, and cannibalization.

The candidate has laid out a broad framework around quantitative and qualitative issues. The components of the framework roughly parallel the 4Cs (in this case, channel, cost, consumers, and competition), and the candidate has indicated that he intends to address at least the most relevant elements in the context of this case. The point is, use whatever structure makes sense to you in the context of the problem you're trying to solve. Don't force business school frameworks if you don't need to-you risk coming across like you're trying too hard and not thinking for yourself. Interviewers will be impressed by your ability to think in a structured and creative way, and not by a knack for regurgitating frameworks.

Nailing the Case

Candidate: To start, let's talk about Rick's Kicks' performance in recent years, and the performance of key channels in the market in total. I'm guessing that Rick's Kicks is currently distributed most broadly in chains and department stores-have you been losing share in those channels? What have been the recent trends surrounding your channels of distribution? How has the mass channel been performing in the footwear segment?

Following the second rule of business strategy cases, the candidate is asking questions aimed at determining the root cause of Rick's Kicks' poor performance in recent years and the channel dynamics at work in the market.

Interviewer: Good questions. You're correct that our brand is primarily distributed in chains and department stores, which currently comprise about 40 percent of total unit sales in the market, and about 50 percent of dollar sales. Four years ago, however, those numbers were 50 percent and 60 percent, respectively. Our core channels have taken a hit in recent years, in large part due to the growth of the mass channel, but our brand has managed to hold its own in terms of market share. We are exactly where we were four years ago, as are almost all of our competitors. The mass channel now accounts for 30 percent of total shoe sales, though only 25 percent of sales is in dollar terms. The mass channel has been growing at about a 10 percent CAGR (compound annual growth rate) over the past four years, and going forward, this trend is expected to continue.

The interviewer is divulging a lot of information quickly, which may indicate both that you are on the right track and that there is a lot of subject matter to cover.

Candidate: Rick's Kicks, then, is holding ground on market share, but is losing sales due to a declining market. In addition, the mass channel is big, and will continue to get bigger. My first reaction is that this opportunity will be a difficult one to pass on. First, though, let's talk briefly about cost. The mass

channel is obviously a lower-cost alternative to your current channels, and consumers have clearly been migrating to mass retailers. Is Rick's Kicks capable of competing in the mass channel from a cost point of view?

The candidate has put forth a preliminary hypothesis, but has stopped short of a recommendation.

Interviewer: Yes, I believe we can compete from a cost point of view. To begin with, mass merchants require less margin than our current customers, which helps. In addition, the products we currently sell are largely high-performance shoes. I think we could readily value engineer our current product to a lower cost. Not to mention the fact that all of our competitors from our current channels have been able to make the economics work.

Again, the interviewer seems to be leading the candidate down a path. Be wary of following blindly into a trap, but if you have the facts to make a recommendation, go for it.

Candidate: That leads me to my next questions around the competitive landscape. What's the composition of the mass channel today from a competitive point of view?

The candidate is probing on the "final C" of the framework he laid out at the outset: competition.

Interviewer: The competitive landscape in the mass channel is as follows: About 40 percent of the shoes sold there are private label brands produced by the retailers themselves. They're the lowest priced shoes on the floor. About 25 percent of the shoes are sold by brands that operate only in the mass channel, and the other 35 percent comprises our competitors' brands and sub-brands. In fact, we're the last remaining major brand not selling in the mass channel.

Again, the interviewer has offered some very powerful information regarding the client's situation.

Candidate: The erosion of Rick's Kicks core channels, combined with the ongoing growth of the mass market, Rick's Kicks' stated ability to manufacture to mass channel cost requirements, and competitors' early and seemingly successful forays into the channel, lead me to believe that Rick's Kicks must enter the mass channel. The key questions that emerge next surround how best to do so. What are the right pricing and branding strategies, and how can Rick's Kicks best minimize cannibalization risk? First, how is Rick's Kicks currently positioned in its core channels of distribution?

The candidate has put a stake in the ground on entering the mass channel. He examined the issue from three points of view, and the facts overwhelmingly supported channel entry. Not one to rest on his laurels, the candidate is off to the races on part two.

Interviewer: In chain stores, Rick's Kicks is a premium offering, priced about $5 to $10 above our closest competitors. In department stores, which are a bit more upscale, our brand is somewhat more mid-range, but still a favorite of many consumers.

Candidate: Clearly, there are always risks to taking any brand down-market. Given your brand's position in its current channels, however, and the facts that private label and mass channel-only brands are prevalent in the mass channel, there seems to be room for your brand at the top end of the spectrum within the mass channel. I see a couple of benefits to such a position. First, you'd continue to command a relative price premium, which would help keep margins healthy and put less pressure on your sourcing and supply chain. Second, it will mitigate, though by no means eliminate, the risk to your brand in your core channels.

The candidate is diving into the critical "how" portion of the question. Given the relative ease with which the interviewer dished out the data earlier, the candidate should expect to invest a good amount of time in this more tactical part of the question.

Interviewer: Okay, so maybe we can carve out a premium positioning. But how do we ensure that we don't lose that position in our core channels when we enter the mass channel? I definitely don't want to simply swap units channel for channel, particularly given that mass channel units are less profitable.

For the first time, the interviewer is challenging the candidate a bit. Perhaps the interviewer has intentionally lured the candidate into thinking the interview would be somewhat of a cakewalk and has now changed tack to test the candidate's cool under fire.

Candidate: Certainly, cannibalization is a serious concern. Is entering the mass channel with an entirely different brand a possibility for Rick's Kicks?

The candidate is not flustered and has decided to use a tried and true strategy. When you sense a bit of defensiveness or aggression, asking a question will often help deflect those feelings more effectively than replying with a statement.

Interviewer: Good question. Actually, it depends on what you mean by "entirely." We're free to create a new brand offering, but the retailer is requiring that its name contain the words "Rick's Kicks." We negotiated hard on that point, but the retailer won't budge. It's a deal breaker.

The interviewer is back in nice and helpful mode again.

Candidate: So the retailer obviously sees a lot of value in the brand equity of Rick's Kicks, and from what I know, it would seem that consumers see that value as well. Given the retailer's conditions, we still have some options. I don't believe that launching the current Rick's Kicks line in the mass channel is a good option. The risk to the brand is too high, current retail customers would likely retaliate, and the price points wouldn't translate anyhow. Instead, Rick's Kicks should consider a sub-brand of some kind. One option would be something like "Rick's Kicks Olympian," which leverages heavily off of the core brand name but also creates differentiation with the "Olympian" addition.

Naming the Case

However, I'd be more comfortable with a brand name like "Swift by Rick's Kicks," or "Fleet Feet, from the makers of Rick's Kick's." These endorsed brands still confer some of the equity of the Rick's Kick's brand, but without leading off with the Rick's Kicks name. Over time, this may allow you to establish a separate brand identity for the mass channel line, and even to drop Rick's Kick's from the name altogether.

Excellent. The candidate walked through a few of the branding options and displayed his comfort in that arena. In addition, he raised for the first time the issue of retail retaliation from current retail customers. It's a good issue to let the interviewer know you're aware of, but in this case it doesn't seem to be a critical issue. Earlier we learned two facts-competitors have maintained their share in core channels while simultaneously entering the mass market-that would seem to indicate retail retaliation is not an immediate risk.

Interviewer: That's extremely helpful; we hadn't thought through the branding options in detail to date.

Case 10

Your client is a major branded skateboard manufacturer that has decided to enter the Brazilian market. Should it license its brand or manage the entry in-house?

This is a common new markets/expansion strategy question, though the licensing element is somewhat of a twist.

Bad Answer

Candidate: I've heard about a lot of companies trying to do business in South America that have lost their shirts down there. The economies are unstable, and the currency is unpredictable. If the company really must enter the Brazilian

market, I'd license the business without a doubt. In any event, my background is in really down-in-the-details manufacturing and operations stuff, not in these fluffier strategy cases.

Obviously not a strong start. Candidates are sometimes surprised by the fact that they receive cases that don't touch on areas of personal expertise. Don't be surprised by this; in fact, expect it. Interviewers want to see if you're capable of stretching beyond comfort zones.

Interviewer: You mentioned other companies that have failed in South America. Maybe we can use them as a starting point to determine if there are applicable lessons from their experiences?

Ahhh, what a friendly interviewer. This candidate may have more than one life . . .

Candidate: Actually, I read about a few in the *Wall Street Journal*, but I don't have a ton of details. Can we talk about throughput instead?

The only throughput measure that's relevant to this candidate is the rate at which his body is about to move through the exit.

Good Answer

Candidate: This is an interesting one. I can't say I'm too familiar with skateboarding personally, but I'm sure I can ask some questions along the way to sort through the issues. This case of course ultimately hinges on the benefits of licensing versus keeping the business in-house for entry into the Brazilian skateboarding market; the decision to enter the market has already been reached. Therefore, it seems that my first step should be to weigh the relative economics of licensing versus the in-house scenario, and see how that comes out. If that's not clear-cut, then we'll want to consider some qualitative issues that may affect the decision, but I think I should hold off on those to see if they prove necessary. To begin with, could you please give me a sense of how a licensing arrangement would work, both organizationally and financially? I want to make sure I'm clear on that before we jump in.

Good start. The candidate has clearly spelled out her approach to the case, and has started with the big picture. In addition, she's not afraid to ask a question about licensing arrangements, a very specific area with which she's not familiar. It's always better to ask the question than to pretend you know things that you don't. Save that until you actually become a consultant.

Interviewer: In a licensing scenario, the client would choose a third-party vendor that would manage the production and sales of its skateboards in Brazil. The client would retain responsibility for designing the product and would have full authority over the use of its brand. Presumably, the vendor the company selected would be one that has deep familiarity and competencies in the Brazilian marketplace. From a financial standpoint, the client would collect a 6 percent royalty on gross sales.

Great. The candidate got what she needed.

Candidate: Thank you. That's helpful. Next, can you please tell me a bit about the skateboard market in the United States? How big is the market, and what is the client's market share?

The data hunt continues.

Interviewer: I don't see why that would be important. The question is about the Brazilian market, not the U.S. market. Did you mean to say Brazil?

The interviewer issues a little bit of a challenge, possibly to test the candidate's persistence, or possibly to signal that she's on the wrong track.

Candidate: I should clarify. I think that understanding just a couple of quick facts about the U.S. market will help me make some assumptions later on about how well the client can expect to do when it enters Brazil.

The candidate holds her ground, sensing that the interviewer is testing her a bit.

Interviewer: Fair enough—that makes sense. I can tell you that the company's market share in the United States is about 5 percent of total units, making it the number three or four player in the market. Unfortunately, I don't have the client's sales data in front of me, so I can't tell you off-hand what the total market size is. You'll have to make an assumption.

So, the interviewer seems to have been testing the candidate's resolve on the previous point. But now a small hurdle has arisen: It seems that a market-sizing question has reared its head inside this broader strategy question. This is not at all uncommon. Just as on the market-sizing questions you've already practiced, make good assumptions, use round numbers, and move on. It's your method, not your number, that counts.

Candidate: Okay. Let's assume that of a total U.S. population of 280 million, about 70 million are age 25 and under, which I imagine is the demographic of most skateboarders. Of those, let's assume that one in seven owns a skateboard, or about 10 million people. My guess would be that most of these people own one skateboard, but that there is certainly a more serious contingent of people who own several. If we assume that it averages out to about 1.5 boards per person, the total number of skateboards would be 15 million. In addition, I think it's fair to assume that a skateboarder might upgrade his board once a year, making the annual market for skateboards in the United States 15 million.

Fair enough. When a market-sizing question is embedded in a broader case, it's usually best to move through it quickly without getting tangled in too many detailed assumptions. After all, it's just one piece of a much bigger puzzle, so don't get bogged down.

Interviewer: Sounds reasonable to me. Let's keep moving.

Candidate: Okay, so if the market for skateboards in the United States is 15 million, and the client has a 5 percent share, this would mean that its annual sales are 750,000 boards. I think that will be a helpful reference point when I begin to think about what the company's "fair share" might be in the Brazilian market. Turning now to …

Interviewer: Fair share? What does that mean? Do you mean that the client will be entitled to the same share it has in the United States in the Brazilian market? But aren't the markets different?

Another challenge—but this candidate seems up to the task.

Candidate: I mean to say that the client's share in the U.S market may serve as a helpful proxy for thinking about how it will perform in Brazil. But in order to validate that hypothesis, I do need to ask a couple of questions about the Brazilian market. How big is that marketplace right now? I imagine it's less mature than the U.S. market. In addition, what does the competitive landscape look like? Are the same brands that compete with the client in the United States also selling in Brazil? Knowing that will help me to figure out whether the "fair share" assumptions I plan to use are valid.

The candidate calmly responds to the interviewer's challenge and clearly explains where she's headed.

Interviewer: The market for skateboards in Brazil is indeed smaller than in the United States, as you say. Last year, about a million boards were sold in Brazil. The market, however, is projected to grow very quickly, which is one of the reasons why the company is interested in it. To your second question, the top two brands in the United States are also the top two in Brazil. Much of U.S. skate culture has made its way to Brazil, and kids there have latched on to the same brands.

Here, the interviewer seems to validate much of the candidate's approach, offering some helpful hints.

Candidate: Great. So Brazil is a small but growing skateboard market that looks a lot like the United States from a competitive standpoint. Let me apply a bit of fair share logic here and see what it tells us. Let's assume for a minute that the client could achieve the same 5 percent share in Brazil. That would imply annual sales of 50,000 skateboards, a pretty small number, especially in comparison with the U.S. business of 750,000. You did mention that the market in Brazil was growing rapidly, but even at a compound annual growth rate of 20 percent, sales would grow to only about 100,000 units in four years, assuming steady market share of 5 percent. In addition, I assume that the retail price of skateboards in Brazil would be substantially lower than in the United States, and would therefore dictate that the skateboards made for sale in Brazil be produced far more cheaply.

So, my initial hunch is that the Brazilian business is a strong candidate for licensing, given its relatively small size in the near term and my assumptions about the amount of investment that would be required for the client to manage the entry in-house. To my last point, are there any existing capabilities or relationships that the client would be able to leverage in entering the market? For example, are there distribution relationships that span both the United States and Brazil? Would the client need to add employees to manage the new business? In addition, I'm wondering whether you know if the company's competitors in Brazil have decided to license their businesses there. That would be interesting to know.

The candidate has done a bit of math that has led her to hypothesize that the size of the Brazilian business may warrant licensing. But she's not yet sure enough to draw a line in the sand and has opted to dig a bit deeper. Floating an initial hypothesis to

Naming the Case

WetFeet®

gauge your interviewer's response can be a smart way to test ideas. Just be careful not to appear like you're fishing for validation; this could signal a lack of confidence.

Interviewer: Good questions. From a capability and relationship standpoint, the client won't have the benefit of very much leverage. The retail landscape in Brazil is very different from the United States, but just as fragmented. So a new sales force would definitely be needed. And you're correct: Retail prices in Brazil are about half of what they are in the United States, so production would need to be cheaper. The company couldn't afford to make the boards by hand as it does in the United States. And lastly, I do know that the number one competitor in Brazil licenses its brand to a third-party vendor.

Candidate: Given what I know, my preliminary recommendation would be in favor of licensing due to the small size of the business and what would seem to be the hefty investment required. From an investment standpoint, I'd be particularly concerned that the client would need to dramatically alter its production process to value-engineer the boards for Brazil. Making them by hand would be difficult to sustain in a substantially lower-priced market. In addition, licensing would potentially mitigate some of the risk of entering a market in a country that has been economically volatile in the past. On the other hand, there are certainly some arguments to be made in favor of keeping the business. For example, if my fair share assumptions actually proved to be conservative, licensing the business could prevent the client from realizing some of its upside. Nonetheless, based on what I know, licensing seems the better approach.

The candidate successfully builds on her previous hypothesis and uses the new information to solidify her position. She also wisely acknowledges a potential counterargument, which is a great way to demonstrate a command of all of the issues surrounding a case.

Interviewer: That seems like a reasonable conclusion. One last question: If this were an actual project, is there anything else you would do before coming to a decision?

Candidate: Good question. The answer is yes. In a real project, it would be critical to build a detailed model to understand the relative economics of licensing and keeping in-house. My analysis was admittedly high-level, and any actual consulting team would need to dive much deeper into the numbers. I would envision building a few potential fair share scenarios for licensing, and run a sensitivity analysis. Ultimately, we'd need to compare the NPV (net present value) of each scenario, using a 6 percent royalty rate for the licensing scenario, and using smart assumptions based on what we know about the market for the in-house scenario.

The candidate acknowledges the limitations of her analysis, limitations that are to be expected in the context of a short case. But she has a clear point of view on what would be required in an actual project scenario. In this part of the case, an MBA candidate would be expected to have a firmer grasp of the economic decision points than an undergraduate or advanced-degree candidate.

Case 11

Your client is a major car manufacturer with significant sales and brand equity. Though the company is doing well, the CEO is looking for incremental opportunities. A major area of concern is that customers' positive interactions with the brand are largely limited to the car-buying experience, which occurs on average once every three years. How would you increase customers' positive interactions with the brand?

This question is part marketing strategy, part growth strategy. Initial indications are that it is a primarily qualitative case that will require some creative, though fact-based, thinking.

Bad Answer

With the last car I bought new, the negative interactions began as soon as I drove the thing off the lot. After a transmission overhaul and a brake replacement, I decided to unload it.

This guy is clearly a joker, but his ridiculous response does raise one point. Try not to let your personal perceptions of a product or a marketplace unduly influence your handling of a case. If you have relevant knowledge or expertise, certainly use it, but stay objective and clear-headed.

Good Answer

Candidate: My initial feeling is that this case will prove to be a lot about marketing and customer relationship management. I think it makes sense to start by mapping out a typical buyer's current experience with the brand, from research to purchase to ownership and then on to the next purchase cycle. I may even go ahead and sketch that cycle on a piece of scratch paper. If I can understand what the customer's current relationship with the brand looks like, hopefully I'll uncover potential points of improvement.

Great start. This is a pretty wide-open case, and there's a risk of jumping into the fray with a bunch of ideas that aren't well-founded. The candidate wisely proposes a structure and has chosen to start by taking a look at the brand through the customer's eyes. After all, this case is about the customer's experiences, so starting from that perspective seems like a sound approach.

Interviewer: Sounds okay to me. Let's get started and see where it leads.

Candidate: There is a lot about the experience of buying and owning a car that is universal across brands. Beginning with the research process, a consumer might start out talking with friends to get their opinions and read publications like *Consumer Reports* to get a feel for what's available. I'm sure that the Internet

is also a key channel for car research these days. I imagine that most consumers narrow down their list of potential cars in these ways, and then once they have a manageable list, begin to visit dealerships and test-drive cars. Outside of online research and third-party reviews, this is likely the customer's first meaningful interaction with the brand. After coming to a decision and navigating what can surely be a difficult and confusing negotiation and purchase process, the customer buys the car and drives it home. Given the frustration many customers feel during the sales process, there may be some opportunities for improvement here, but from your question it seems that the case is focused largely on the post-purchase phase.

Interviewer: Yes. What happens then?

The interviewer may be expressing a bit of impatience, as the candidate is being a bit deliberate about setting up his analysis. Don't get flustered; often, interviewers are giving cases all day, and at a certain point, it's not hard to see how they could get a bit tired from all of the repetition. Stay calm, and if you sense this, try to cut to the chase. But don't get so rushed that you lose sight of your structure or skip over key parts of your analysis.

Candidate: Once the customer is off the lot, there can be significant gaps in what I'll call "customer touch points" with the brand. Sure, the customer is driving the car every day, and there is probably some loyalty to the brand that is reinforced each time the driver gets behind the wheel, but it's a much different kind of interaction than being at the dealership. And there are plenty of opportunities for negative interaction, and reading between the lines; I imagine that this is one of the things that the client is concerned about. For example, every six months or so an insurance premium comes due, which can certainly be expensive. In addition, things go wrong with cars, and anything from a minor fix to a major repair can have a damaging effect to the brand. So this is the area in which I need to focus. A couple of questions that come to mind are,

first, can the company somehow transform experiences like insurance and repair into more positive ones, and, second, are there new touch points in the cycle that it can insert to create more positive relationships with the consumer?

It's taken the candidate a little while to warm up, but he seems to have hit upon some of the potentially negative points in the ownership cycle.

Interviewer: Okay. But how are you going to make insurance and repair positive experiences? That seems like a bit of a stretch.

Candidate: True, it's certainly difficult to imagine. And I'm not sure that insurance and repair would ever be truly positive experiences, but maybe they could be less negative for starters. For example, what if the company offered free or discounted vehicle check-ups at their dealerships every 25,000 miles? Customers might save some money through preventive maintenance, and the program would give the company an opportunity to reinforce its relationship by bringing customers back to its dealerships. Or it could affiliate itself with selected insurance and repair companies and offer incentives to its customers through a joint partnership. Customers could earn points by using these partner providers, and apply those points toward the purchase of their next vehicle, or toward accessories for their current cars.

The candidate does a good job of responding to the challenge from the interviewer. Remember, this is a case about ideas and your ability to generate them and back them up with reasonable assumptions and assertions. Of course any of these ideas would need to be carefully analyzed before the company would implement them, but that's not what you're here to do. Be creative, and ground your creativity in credible assumptions.

Interviewer: Those are interesting ideas. It sounds like you're talking about some kind of loyalty program. If so, what would you envision some of the guiding principles of the program to be? How else might you promote the program?

Positive sign—the interviewer has latched on to the candidate's ideas and is probing a bit further.

Candidate: You're right; I am talking about a loyalty program. Programs like this have of course proven to be successful in other industries-airlines come to mind first. Not that they don't have problems of their own, but their mileage programs are certainly models for loyalty programs. In terms of guiding principles, I think that the core principle of a loyalty program is that it should create a self-reinforcing cycle. By which I mean that the points that a customer earns should become "currency" that encourages a future transaction with the parent brand or one of its key partners. If the company were to create such a program, the customer should be able to apply his or her points to the purchase of a brand product. In terms of other ways to promote the program, I'd encourage the company to consider a credit card as a part of the loyalty offering. I personally have a gas card and an airline card in my wallet at the moment, and I know that credit cards like these have been quite successful in recent years. A branded credit card would serve the dual purpose of reinforcing a positive experience with the brand as consumers earn points and increasing the likelihood of a repeat purchase.

Interviewer: A credit card is a good idea. Is there anything else?

Candidate: I'm also thinking about the day-to-day driving experience, as this is certainly the most substantive and significant part of the brand relationship. As I said earlier, there is some benefit each time the customer drives the car, but I think that in-car options like the OnStar system, for example, could enhance the quality of the brand relationship. Value-added services like roadside assistance and driving directions go above and beyond the typical expectations of a vehicle, and therefore may become an ongoing source of positive reinforcement.

The candidate continues to stretch his thinking and offer creative responses. Again, whether these ideas would pay off would remain to be seen. Nonetheless, the candidate is responding to the call of duty by having creative yet credible answers at the ready.

Interviewer: Those are all reasonable ideas. There's just one more thing. I mentioned at the outset that this is a brand with considerable equity and is in fact doing quite well. Would those facts lead you to consider anything else?

The interviewer seems to have something in mind that the candidate didn't touch upon. This is likely one of those areas that would be considered "extra credit," and a potentially important differentiator from the pack. Nail these parts of the interview, and you'll be in good shape.

Candidate: Now that you mention it, the company could probably put its strong brand equity to work by exploring opportunities in other markets, either directly related to cars or even somewhat further afield. My own credit card example calls to mind financial services. One could see where the brand attributes that serve a car company well—reliability, trust, safety—would also be transferable to financial services. Whatever the potential markets might be, the company's strong financial position coupled with its powerful brand could make it a candidate for product line expansion.

Excellent! The candidate has seized on a path that flows directly from the interviewer's last question. This guy may be cut out for consulting after all.

Interviewer: Great job on a tough, open-ended case.

Case 12

Your firm is involved in a competitive bid with two other consulting firms for a project with a major carbonated soda manufacturer. The company is considering entering the U.S. bottled water market, and will be hiring a

consulting firm to help it assess the opportunity. **The partner leading the proposal effort has asked you to assist her in preparing a presentation for the company's executives. How would you structure the presentation? What issues would you address?**

This is a pretty standard market-entry question made somewhat unique by the presentation/proposal element. You'd be likely to find a question like this at all candidate levels.

Bad Answers

- Sounds pretty tricky to me. I'm not sure I'd really want to buy a bottled water product from a company that makes soda. Doesn't seem like a very logical fit to me. It just seems like bottled water is too much of a stretch for a brand that is fundamentally about carbonated soda.
  There's an important issue embedded in there somewhere: the feasibility of brand extension in this case. But the case didn't specify that the brand name would necessarily be used for any bottled water launch, and the candidate has relied on a personal bias to make a broad conclusion.

- Absolutely. Bottled water is a great market. Costs are low, and manufacturers are able to command impressive price premiums by creating brands that are about status and prestige. The company should definitely enter the market.
  How does the candidate know bottled water is a great market? Is success in bottled water really as easy as the candidate suggests? Does the success of other brands necessarily mean certain profits for the company? The candidate has made too many unsupported assumptions.

Good Answer

Candidate: Given that I'm helping a partner with a presentation, I think it will be especially important here to think through an appropriate structure. Some key areas I'll want to consider are market size, competition, distribution, and price. Using Porter's Five Forces crossed my mind, but on second thought I think that a 5Cs framework may work better here. I don't want to seem overly "frameworky," but again, given the nature of the assignment, it seems critical that there be a clear and manageable structure. I'll want to think about the

following areas: consumers, competition, cost, channel, and capabilities. And since we're working through a proposal here, I think the important thing is to highlight the areas our team would focus on should we win the bid, not specific recommendations.

The candidate has done a solid job of outlining what he believes to be the "scope" of the interview—that is, calling out key issues, not making detailed recommendations. This is a proposal, not a final presentation. If you make all of your recommendations here, there wouldn't be much reason to hire you, now would there? One additional thing to note: The candidate made a fairly overt effort here to disclaim his use of frameworks. While you should certainly be wary of coming across like an audio book of a business school text, if it makes sense to use a framework, feel free to use it, and don't get wrapped up in apologizing for it, as this candidate does.

Interviewer: All right, let's get started. You mentioned consumers?

Candidate: Yes, consumers. The consumer lens of the presentation should reflect a couple of different areas. First, it would be critical to lay out the size of the market for bottled water in the United States. How much of the stuff are consumers buying each year, in units and dollars? Is there a consumer segmentation that makes sense to think about? For example, along demographic lines of gender, age, and income? Or maybe a behavioral segmentation would be helpful as well. How much bottled water is bought for casual consumption around the house or the office, versus for use in exercise or sports? And how does the market break out between personal and business consumers?

Good start. Again, this case is largely about outlining the approach you'd take if hired by the company. Each of the questions the candidate asks may take the shape of a page, or a part of a page, in the presentation he is helping with. Also, consumer segmentation will generally perk up the ears of a consultant.

Interviewer: I agree. All of that would be important to determine. Keep going.

Candidate: As for competition, I'd certainly want to put together a market map that lays out the competitive landscape. Who are the key competitors, and what are their market shares? An assessment of the competition may also uncover some interesting insights from a benchmarking standpoint. Have other carbonated beverage manufacturers entered the bottled water marketplace? If so, what was their approach to launching a water offering? Was it successful? I think it would be interesting to include a competitive "deep dive" or two to highlight a success case that we could learn from, and maybe a less successful case as well. My gut tells me that the competition filter will be a really important one here. Personal experience tells me that there are a lot of bottled water brands out there, so the market could prove to be saturated. That remains to be seen.

The candidate uses the competition filter to hit on a couple of key issues. First, market share. That's an obvious one that you'll always want to think about in the context of a market-entry case. Who are the major players and how big are they? Second, the candidate also thought about a benchmarking path, which can be very useful in a case like this. Consultants spend a lot of time benchmarking, trying to learn from the successes, failures, and business practices of selected companies (kind of like you may have done in business school . . . a thousand times).

Interviewer: Okay, I agree with you on the market share point. We'll definitely need to know that. But the benchmarking stuff? We have limited resources to put toward this proposal—is that really a necessary piece of the presentation?

Candidate: I fully appreciate the limited resources available here. But I do believe that a benchmarking could prove to be extremely useful to the company as it considers if and how to enter the marketplace. Certainly, all of these analyses would have to be prioritized against our team's capacity.

The candidate has decided to hold his ground. Interviewers will often test your willingness to stick to your guns, so if you think you have a good idea, hold to it. But also be attuned to strong hints from the interviewer. After a couple of inquiries on the same subject, you may want to start to think about following where the interviewer is leading you.

Interviewer: Fair enough. What's next?

Candidate: Next, I'd want to think about cost. In the cost bucket, I'd include retail and wholesale price with an eye to trends in the marketplace. In addition, it will be important to overlay the competition and cost filters to understand price dynamics at the brand level. For instance, my hunch is that private label brands are playing an increasingly important role in the market, particularly in grocery stores and mass merchants. Typically, the emergence of private label competitors signals the commoditization of a marketplace and a commensurate drop in price. My hunch is that brands like Evian, which largely invented the bottled water category several years ago, have lost significant share and price premium as lower-priced competitors have come into play. If the bottled water market is indeed experiencing these kinds of deflationary trends, that would be extremely important to explore, as it could significantly impact the economics surrounding the company's decision. We'd need to determine whether the company would be able to stem the tide of price pressure (if it exists) in the market and command any kind of a premium. If not, it could be in for a price war.

Here, the candidate does a great job of posing some key questions around cost, which he perceives to be a critical lever. The candidate offers some reasonable hypotheses, but is careful to note that they are just that—hypotheses. All of his suppositions would of course require further data to confirm or refute.

Interviewer: It seems like you're saying that the bottled water market may not be that attractive for the company? If prices are dropping and bottled water is becoming a commodity, maybe it's not the best market to enter? Is that right?

Candidate: Not necessarily. You're right, my hypothesis is that the company may encounter some difficulties from competitive and price standpoints. But I don't necessarily believe that those factors alone make bottled water an unattractive market. In any event, there's certainly quite a bit of analysis to do before any of these questions get answered. In addition, I think that the company may also have some things going for it that could counterbalance some of the potential downside of a bottled water offering. For example, let's think about channel dynamics. We'd certainly want to know how the market breaks out from a distribution standpoint—where is bottled water sold? How many units and dollars move through mass merchants, grocery stores, warehouse clubs, gas stations, and all of the other categories of outlets through which bottled water is sold? I'd then want to overlay that information with a snapshot of the company's current distribution model. My sense is that there will be a good deal of overlap. I know from my own experience that the company is sold through all major grocery stores and mass merchants, and my hypothesis is that those channels account for a large percentage of bottled water sales. So the company would probably be able to leverage its existing sales and distribution relationships in order to launch a bottled water product quickly and widely.

Excellent. The candidate responded in a fact-based and thoughtful way to the interviewer, who was clearly trying to push him down a particular path. Again, the candidate has made some sound assumptions based on the information available to him and has proposed some analyses that will definitely be important to the company's assessment.

Interviewer: So distribution could be a positive. That makes sense. Is that all?

Candidate: The last area I'd want to think about is capability: Does the company have any pre-existing processes, systems, or people in place that it could leverage to launch bottled water more cheaply and effectively. I think the answer to that question is likely to be "yes." The company probably has a large network of bottlers that could likely be leveraged for a bottled water offering. In addition, current relationships in areas like packaging and advertising could potentially be used to drive costs down. These certainly aren't cut-and-dried issues, and we'd need to take a deeper look when any potential project kicked off. It is possible, for example, that there actually aren't any cost savings in packaging if the bottling is currently done in glass and aluminum, and the water offering would be plastic. Nonetheless, whether it's through spare capacity in bottling facilities or raw materials, I imagine that points of leverage will surface.

The candidate does a good job of raising questions that, while unanswerable now, would be important to address.

Interviewer: Great. But I think you've left out one element of the analysis. What about brand? Are there any issues to think about there?

Candidate: You're right, brand is important—I guess I may have forgotten it because it didn't start with a "C." Anyway, the company will need to think about its core brand's extendibility—that is, will a brand name associated with a carbonated product play well in a health-oriented water market? On the one hand, you could argue that it wouldn't, that soda simply has too many unhealthy connotations to drive sales in a water market. On the other hand, the company is a popular brand with considerable equity, and I can certainly understand that the company would want to put its brand name to work as it enters a new category. One option I'd consider would be a sub-brand of some kind. It could be possible to leverage the brand name but in an endorsement capacity. For example, "Pure Rainwater from the makers of . . ." Or maybe just subtly place the company corporate logo somewhere on the bottle.

Good recovery. The candidate left out one part of the analysis that the interviewer thought was important. Once asked, the candidate attempted a joke and then raised some of the key issues surrounding the company brand and bottled water.

Interviewer: Nice job.

Resume Questions

Case 13

What would you contribute to the community of our firm outside of your work?

This question is designed to reveal a bit about who the candidate is as a person. Come to your interview prepared to talk about leadership, community involvement, and interests. After all, your interviewer may someday spend 70 hours a week holed up with you in a paper factory in Pocatello. The time will pass a lot faster if you're interesting.

Bad Answer

I hear you consultants work 70-hour weeks. Where do you find the time for anything but work? In business school, I was in a bunch of really interesting clubs, and I think that pattern would manifest itself in consulting as well. I'd be up to pitch in for any kind of extracurricular activity.

It's best to be specific about your past experience and your likely future involvement in activities at the firm. Relaying a long list of business school clubs won't necessarily

separate a candidate from peers; it's critical to bring your personal involvement to life. For example, maybe you were the chairperson of a charity auction at your school, and you struck deals with several local vendors who agreed to donate meals, plane tickets, and hotel rooms to the auction. Whatever your example may be, think through how you can highlight your personal commitment and accomplishments.

Good Answer

Candidate: Finding the right balance between work and life and ensuring that I participate in the broader community have always been important to me. At previous jobs, at school, and in my personal life, I've made a consistent effort to contribute to my communities, and I'm confident that I'd be an active member of your community as well. Let me give you a few examples.

The candidate does a good job of confidently responding to the question, and even seems to lay out a rough framework for her approach-work, school, and personal life. A framework is by no means required for these questions, but coherence is always helpful.

Candidate: In my job before business school at a start-up, I initiated and organized a food drive for local homeless people during the holiday season. I chose a local food bank to work with, and in November I began soliciting donations from fellow employees through e-mails and flyers in the office. I placed some empty bins in the lobby for people to put food in, and eventually the program took on a life of its own. My colleagues really rallied around the idea, and we ultimately collected several hundred pounds of canned goods for the local food bank. I'd actively seek out opportunities to participate in similar programs at your firm. While in school, I was involved in a broad range of activities, but focused primarily on student government. As vice president of my class, I was responsible for a wide range of events, including social gatherings and community fundraisers. I enjoy taking on those types of positions and would look for opportunities to do so within your firm.

The candidate presents a succinct and thoughtful answer. It's important to toe the line between portraying yourself as actively involved and annoyingly omnipresent. Your interviewer surely knows that there are hundreds of clubs available at college or business school, many of which primarily involve drinking beer and throwing a Frisbee. So be careful to hit the high points and focus on the activities that were truly important to you and where your involvement made a difference. Finally, be specific. Strive to ground your answer in tangible details. Doing so will lend credibility to your response and bring your personality to life.

Candidate: Lastly, I know from friends of mine who work at your firm that your company is a strong supporter of cancer research. Many of my friends who work with you have participated in Race for the Cure on a company-sponsored team. In addition, I recently read in a non-profit journal in one of my classes about an operational efficiency project your firm helped a large cancer research organization with. I've participated in Race for the Cure for the past few years and would be thrilled to do so again next year with a team of colleagues.

Brownie points! The candidate has obviously done her research just by talking with friends. Through these conversations, the candidate learned that the firm she's interviewing with supports a cause that is also close to her heart. Race for the Cure provided the candidate with a great opportunity to highlight one way in which her past personal involvement with a non-profit would intersect with her future participation in the community life of the firm.

Case 14

How would your last supervisor describe you if I called for a reference? What would he or she say about your performance? What might he or she say you could have done better?

This is a fundamentally a question about strengths and weaknesses—we mean, development opportunities. This is one fairly common type of "resume case," and you also might find it asked in a slightly different way. For example, "I see you used to work in corporate strategy at Clorox. Tell me about a project you worked on and its outcome. Describe what you would do differently if you had to do that project again." This is a very similar question to the one we've asked; preparing for one should allow you to tackle either.

Bad Answer

My last supervisor and I disagreed on a lot of issues—would it be possible for us to talk about my job before the most recent one? I had a much better relationship with my supervisor at the earlier job. My last supervisor was a bad micromanager and a worse communicator.

You're going to have to answer the question that's asked of you, even if you'd prefer to answer another one. If you encounter a situation like this, try to think of a way to spin your conflicts with your boss in a way that will impress your interviewer. For example, maybe your boss was very difficult at the outset, but with strong communication and persistence you managed to improve the relationship and make it productive.

Good Answer

Candidate: Most recently, I worked as an analyst in the marketing department of a software company. The company was established enough to have a steady flow of capital, but also young enough that new processes and opportunities were continually emerging. I think that my last supervisor would tell you that I

was analytically rigorous, persistent, and team-oriented. I think that she would say that I was adaptive enough to function in an environment that was simultaneously established and entrepreneurial, and that I was an enjoyable person to have on the team.

The candidate does a nice job of briefly laying out what he perceives to be key strengths his supervisor would hit upon. He doesn't rattle off a laundry list, but instead chooses to focus on a few key traits that he can back up with concrete examples. In addition, the areas he has chosen to highlight are certainly prerequisites for a successful career in consulting. Wherever possible, try to highlight skills and traits that are likely to fit the profile of your desired role, but be careful not to force it. Be yourself.

Candidate: The company sold project management software to companies across a broad range of industries. When I joined the company, we had about a dozen clients. Most of our marketing efforts were centered on direct appeals to senior technical managers. For example, we sent a lot of direct-mail packets describing our product offering and its potential benefits. Response rates on these types of mailers were fairly low. After a few visits to trade shows and multiple conversations with IT staff at various firms, it became clear to me that while senior IT managers were the ultimate decision makers on big software purchases, more junior employees were extremely influential in the decision process. I approached my boss with a proposal that we dive a bit deeper into the software purchase process by designing a survey of IT workers of varying seniority in multiple industries. My boss agreed, and the research ultimately proved the critical importance of the advice of less senior staff in the software purchase process. Following this project, we shifted a good deal of our direct marketing efforts to more junior employees, and we found that their impressions of our product did flow upstream to their managers. I was involved as the representative from the marketing department on a cross-functional team charged with overhauling the marketing materials for more

junior employees. The team included people from sales, our internal IT department, and communications. That part of the project was brief, but I very much enjoyed working with the team and helping to execute on the insights we'd gathered. I'm confident that the team-centered environment of consulting is one I'd thrive in.

The candidate has presented a concrete example that highlights the traits he mentioned as key positives. He managed to find one succinct example that hit upon analytic rigor, persistence, and team orientation. Whether you use one anecdote or several, strive to be as specific and illustrative as possible.

Candidate: In terms of things I could have done better, I think my boss would tell you that I could have been more assertive about taking on a leadership-oriented role on the cross-functional team I was a part of. I was a bit unsure of how I'd be viewed by the team, being a somewhat junior employee. Looking back, however, it occurs to me that the team was seeking a bit of guidance at the outset, and that I would have been welcomed in a leadership role, especially since I'd been the person driving most of the work on the issue. Taking a more formal leadership role would have allowed me to focus on my people management and presentation skills, areas in which I've not had a lot of experience to date. I'm confident I can address these issues over time, however. I'm typically comfortable in leadership positions, and because I know that effective presentations are a crucial part of being a successful consultant, I would devote myself early on to ensuring that my presentation skills were where they needed to be. In addition, I'm confident that my team-oriented and personable style would help me transition smoothly into the role of an associate/analyst and ultimately a project manager.

The candidate remembered to come back to the question of what he could have done better, and talks about what he sees as his development needs. (In the same way that

some consulting firms refer to their sales efforts as "client cultivation," "development needs" is consultant-speak for weaknesses). Here, the candidate expresses a commitment and an eagerness to work on his stated development areas.

Case 15

I see you used to work in product management at the Lee Jeans division of VF Corporation. Describe for me how your product was positioned in the marketplace. What would you say is the biggest challenge facing the Lee brand in the next five years? If you were the CEO, what would you to do meet that challenge?

These types of resume cases, in which an interviewer essentially designs a case around a specific part of your background, are quite common. Your goal should be to convey with clarity and confidence that you have a strong command of the issues facing the company—you worked there, after all—as well as an ability to extract key facts and communicate them clearly to a non-expert audience.

Bad Answer

To be honest, I was in product management, and your question is more for the strategy folks. I could tell you a lot about our source base and production processes, though. We're facing a lot of challenges there as well.

Regardless of your position within your former company, your interviewer will expect that you have a handle on the nature of its business and the key issues it faces. Confessing that you lack an understanding of the broader context in which you were working for a period of several years isn't a strong indicator of curiosity or perspective.

Good Answer

Candidate: Lee Jeans are positioned primarily as a mid-tier brand in our core channel of distribution, national chains like JC Penney and Kohl's. Lee fit in the

middle of the price spectrum, between private label brands on the low end and a brand like Levi's on the high end. Lee approaches the market with a sub-brand portfolio stance. For example, Lee Pipes was targeted at boys and Lee Dungarees at a teen and college consumer. Other sub-brands were positioned to target more discrete market segments, and VF has had considerable success with its segmentation strategy. Though Lee was a mid-range brand, it possesses high name recognition and brand equity, and is a number one or two player in most categories in which it competes.

The candidate concisely answers the first part of the question about positioning, addressing price, channel, and portfolio strategy. Again, the point here is not to overwhelm your interviewer with nuance and detail. Focus on hitting the key points and move on.

Candidate: I would argue that the primary challenges faced by Lee are external rather than internal. VF is widely regarded as having one of the most sophisticated supply chains and leanest cost structures in the apparel business. In addition, though Lee doesn't make designer jeans, I think it has a deep understanding of who its consumer is, and successfully designs for that person. Externally, though, Lee faces a difficult set of issues. The jeans category is becoming increasingly commoditized, driven by the ongoing migration of apparel sales to value retailers, namely Wal-Mart, which now has the world's largest apparel business at more than $25 billion per year. Within a couple of years, as many as four in ten pairs of jeans sold in the United States will be sold at Wal-Mart. The Lee brand, with the exception of a small endorser role, is purposely not available at Wal-Mart, though other brands in the VF portfolio are. Therefore, Lee does not have access to the largest and fastest-growing segment of the market. A key challenge, then, is for Lee to find ways to grow its business and maintain its price points in core channels as Wal-Mart continues to attempt to steal share and push down prices in the overall market.

This candidate obviously knows Lee's business, and also shows her broader understanding of the total jeans market and the VF corporate portfolio. She includes a couple of key statistics that add credibility to her story without bogging her down in too much detail.

Candidate: To meet these challenges, Lee must continue to focus on two areas: product innovation and brand equity. Product innovation, albeit within the range of its core consumers' tastes, will be critical to Lee's ability to differentiate its product from value channel offerings and maintain its price premium versus Wal-Mart and private label brands. Fundamentally, Lee must continue to give consumers real reasons to spend more on its product to keep them from trading down. Finally, I would also invest in shoring up brand equity even further, as Lee did successfully in recent years with its Buddy Lee ad campaign. Building equity with younger consumers will be especially critical as those segments are expected to be the primary drivers of growth in the marketplace in the coming years.

The candidate offers two suggestions for addressing the challenges that face the Lee brand, and she does so succinctly and assuredly. We're sure this consulting firm will be as happy to have her on the team as Lee Jeans likely was.

WetFeet's Insider Guide Series

Ace Your Case! The WetFeet Insider Guide to Consulting Interviews
Ace Your Case II: Fifteen More Consulting Cases
Ace Your Case III: Practice Makes Perfect
Ace Your Case IV: The Latest and Greatest
Ace Your Interview! The WetFeet Insider Guide to Interviewing
Beat the Street: The WetFeet Insider Guide to Investment Banking Interviews
Getting Your Ideal Internship
Get Your Foot in the Door! Landing the Job Interview
Job Hunting A to Z: The WetFeet Insider Guide to Landing the Job You Want
Killer Consulting Resumes!
Killer Cover Letters and Resumes!
Killer Investment Banking Resumes!
Negotiating Your Salary and Perks
Networking Works!: The WetFeet Insider Guide to Networking

Career and Industry Guides

Accounting
Advertising and Public Relations
Asset Management and Retail Brokerage
Biotech and Pharmaceuticals
Brand Management
Health Care
Human Resources
Computer Software and Hardware
Consulting for Ph.D.s, Lawyers, and Doctors
Industries and Careers for MBAs
Industries and Careers for Undergrads
Information Technology
Investment Banking
Management Consulting
Marketing and Market Research

Non-Profits and Government Agencies
Oil and Gas
Real Estate
Sports and Entertainment
Top 20 Biotechnology and Pharmaceutical Firms
Top 25 Consulting Firms
Top 25 Financial Services Firms
Top 20 Law Firms
Venture Capital

Company Guides

Accenture
Bain & Company
Bear Stearns
Booz Allen Hamilton
The Boston Consulting Group
Cap Gemini Ernst & Young
Citigroup
Credit Suisse First Boston
Deloitte Consulting
Goldman Sachs
IBM Business Consulting Services
JPMorgan Chase
Lehman Brothers
McKinsey & Company
Merrill Lynch
Monitor Group
Morgan Stanley